If . . . Then . . . Curriculum: Assessment-Based Instruction, Grade 3

Lucy Calkins with Julia Mooney and Colleagues from the Teachers College Reading and Writing Project

Photography by Peter Cunningham

HEINEMANN ◆ PORTSMOUTH, NH

firsthand
An imprint of Heinemann
361 Hanover Street
Portsmouth, NH 03801–3912
www.heinemann.com

Offices and agents throughout the world

The authors and publisher wish to thank those who have generously given premission to reprint borrowed material:

Quote by Roald Dahl, reprinted by permission of David Higham Associates.

Cataloging-in-Publication data is on file with the Library of Congress.

ISBN-13: 978-0-325-04813-0
ISBN-10: 0-325-04813-4

Production: Elizabeth Valway, David Stirling, and Abigail Heim
Cover and interior designs: Jenny Jensen Greenleaf
Series includes photographs by Peter Cunningham, Nadine Baldasare, and Elizabeth Dunford
Composition: Publishers' Design and Production Services, Inc.
Manufacturing: Steve Bernier

Printed in the United States of America on acid-free paper
17 16 15 14 13 ML 3 4 5

Contents

PART TWO: Differentiating Instruction for Individuals and Small Groups: If . . . Then . . . Conferring Scenarios

Introduction

Third-Grade Writers and Planning Your Year

WHEN MY COLLEAGUES AND I help school systems improve writing instruction or when we lead courses in teaching writing for networks and organizations, we often find that people assume the work will be divided into a K–3 section and a 4–5/6 section. Time and again, we say, "Actually, when it comes to the teaching of writing, the dividing line comes between second- and third-graders. There is a world of difference between teaching writing to second-graders and teaching writing to third-graders, and that difference comes from the fact that most third-graders seem substantially different, as writers, than most second-graders."

UNDERSTAND WAYS THAT EXPECTATIONS, TOOLS, AND TIMETABLES ARE DIFFERENT NOW THAT WRITERS ARE THIRD-GRADERS

Think of a second-grade writing workshop. The children write on special paper that contains a place for drawing and a place for pictures. They churn out one book, then another, then another. Their writing process is fairly simple: they think of a topic, they draw and story-tell or teach, or argue it, and then they write it. Afterward, they may reread and fix up parts that have problems. Then, onward.

By third grade, in contrast, we channel children to write at least a good deal of their work in writer's notebooks. If they are writing narrative writing, students write a bunch of page-long entries, then choose one to make into literature. That one piece of writing requires a lot of work: planning, storytelling, studying a mentor text, time-lining, drafting. Once the draft is written, the writing will require revision, and this may mean writing a new draft on another sheet of paper.

This means that for third-graders, the writing process is vastly more elongated, which can mean that students are able to be more deliberate and plan more at junctures throughout the writing process. Third-graders are taught ways to start a text, plan a text, structure a text, reread a text, revise a text, and so on. They are given a whole new set of tools for writing, starting with a writer's notebook and including booklets or folders for holding bits and pieces of information and opinion writing. Watch many third-graders work, and you will hear them almost talking to themselves, saying things like, "Now I will write a draft, fast and furious," and "Now I will read this over and add details."

The new time frames for writing and new tools support third-graders working through the stages of the writing process in increasingly deliberate, planned, purposeful ways, and when this works well, the difference between what third-graders and fourth-graders do as writers is not large. That is, third-graders, like fourth-graders, can collect several leads or introductions, choose among them, work on alternative plans for a piece, choosing among those, and so on.

SO WHAT DOES THAT MEAN FOR CHILDREN ENTERING THIRD GRADE WITH EXCEPTIONALLY LOW SKILL LEVELS?

As a teacher of third-graders, you need to keep in mind that some third-graders will find the elongated process of writing just too much. They can get bogged down in the forest and lose sight of the trees. For example, if these youngsters are coached to try writing several leads, they may, in the process of doing so, entirely forget the original topic and plan. Consequently, these youngsters may end up writing leads for entirely different pieces, rather than for the piece at hand. They may be coached to write another draft, and the new draft may actually be just an entirely different piece—perhaps better, perhaps worse—but either way, the point is that some third-graders have a hard time wrapping their mental arms around the more elaborated, elongated process that works well for other third-graders.

The length of the page, like the elongated process, can also bog down third-graders who have exceptionally low skill levels. While third-graders who are on track as writers will be able to produce a page of writing in one sitting by the end of third grade, some of your third-graders enter the year producing far less than that, becoming paralyzed in the face of long sheets of notebook paper, producing very little (and usually writing whatever they do write in crabbed, tiny letters).

So you may ask, then, "How can I be sure my students have the foundation that they need for success with the third-grade curriculum as it is laid out in the four Units of Study books?" That's an important question, and I'm not entirely sure of the answer because the real issue revolves around your students' readiness to learn from instruction, to take it, and run with it. The truth is that the third-grade books have taken widely diverse classrooms of youngsters from where they are and gotten them started in a writing workshop. Thousands of teachers have taught the unit that is captured in *Crafting True Stories* to students who are brand new to the writing workshop, and the results are usually hold-your-hat astonishing. We hear all the time from teachers who say, "If I didn't see this with my own eyes, I would never have believed it."

On the other hand, when my colleagues and I work in high-need classrooms, helping third-grade teachers launch writing workshops with third-graders who sometimes are novices not only with a writing workshop but also with writing, we certainly are accustomed to seeing some children work as if with blinders on whatever piece of the process teachers put before them on a given day, losing sight of the goal they are working toward and of a larger sense that they are making something. Those children would probably benefit from starting the year with what we think of as a second-grade writing workshop, where kids write directly into a draft that looks very like the book they will eventually publish, with pages that contain twelve to fifteen lines and a small space for a quick sketch, and where the expectation is that a youngster will write and then revise (with flaps, added or resequenced pages, and so on) half a dozen pieces within a month.

If your students enter third grade with little experience writing (or working within the Common Core State Standards [CCSS] expectations for narrative, information, and opinion writing), the truth is that the choice of which second-grade unit you teach is less important than the fact that you might be wise to delay for a month students' move into writer's notebooks, with all the expectations that accompany that move.

HOW WILL THE ON-DEMAND ASSESSMENTS HELP YOU ADJUST YOUR CURRICULUM?

You'll want to conduct an on-demand narrative writing assessment, of course. You can find prompts for these on-demand assessments in the book *Writing Pathways: Performance Assessments and Learning Progression, K–5.* We find that at the start of the school year, youngsters are rusty from the summer, so before you conduct the assessment, you probably want to show children some narrative writing that other third-graders have written, asking them to tell you what they notice the author has done. This gives you a quick sense of the goals they are accustomed to working toward and the language they use for those goals. Meanwhile, this inquiry reminds those children who enter third grade with a background in writing what they know.

After two or three days or so in which you immerse your children in narrative writing, you'll ask them to take fifty minutes and write the best personal narrative they can write. You may want to make this on-demand writing feel celebratory—give your students a chance to show off what they know about narrative writing. You might say, "I'm really eager to understand what you can do as writers, so before you do anything else, please spend today writing the very best personal narrative—the best Small Moment story—of one particular time in your life. You'll have fifty minutes to write this true story of one small moment. Write in a way that shows me all that you know about how to do this kind of writing." You may also want to spell out some of your expectations for narrative writing—see the prompt we provide in *Writing Pathways: Performance Assessments and Learning Progressions, K–5.*

While the students are writing, be sure you don't coach them. Don't remind them to write with details or to focus. You want to see what they do in a hands-off situation—and frankly, you want to be in a position to show great growth from this starting point. That means you'll really want to find out what their starting points are, so you can extend their skills. The data you collect by doing an on-demand writing assessment will be invaluable as you take the time to learn what your students already know and can do. When you sit with the writing the students produce, brace yourself! The first thing to keep in mind is that the third-grade expectations are for the far end of the school year (and frankly, they are not necessarily expectations for a fifty-minute on-demand writing time, anyhow). You are absolutely *not* expecting children to enter third grade producing on-demand writing that is at the end-of-third-grade level. You should feel very pleased if many of your children are somewhere in the ballpark of writing at the second-grade level (because that means they haven't had summer slippage and are starting the third grade just about where they should be). If your children are writing narratives that are in the midway range between first and second grade, they are probably well positioned to participate in the third-grade units. On the other hand, if some of their narratives are at or below the first-grade level, you might decide to postpone the first unit in the series and first teach a precursor narrative unit, one that has actually been designed more as a second-grade unit but can provide a stepladder to prepare your students for the rigors of the third-grade curriculum. If you give these students a month or two where it's not only the minilessons that you teach that are supportive, but where the pace you expect and the tools you provide may be more similar to what we normally suggest for second-graders, this will work well. I describe the options you might take in more detail in a later section of this introduction: "Developing an If . . . Then . . . Curriculum Based on Your Children's Needs."

You may find that your students are able to produce fairly strong narratives during the on-demand but that they don't do some of the specific things that are highlighted in the Units of Study books. That is, they may write a long, cohesive story, with a beginning, middle, and end, with evidence of elaboration and transitions, but they don't keep the story focused or include dialogue. This is simply a matter of instruction, suggesting that the upcoming third-grade books will serve these children very well. That is, it is certainly not necessary for children to have progressed through our K–2 units of study for them to be ready for the third-grade units.

Remember that you will give the assessments not only to decide whether to proceed with the existing units, but also so that you can track students' progress. By capturing the data representing what writers can do at the start of your work with a kind of writing, you put yourself in a position to show parents and others all the ways your students have grown as writers over the course of the year. For example, in your autumn parent-teacher conferences, you will want to bring the writing a learner did on the first day of school and contrast it with the writing he or she did recently. Having the before and after comparison allows you to illuminate the growth students have (and have not yet) made.

Because you will be using the on-demands as data to track growth, it is especially imperative that this is a hands-off assessment. Resist the temptation to scaffold kids' work during this assessment.

The job is not just to give these on-demand assessments, but also to take seriously the challenge of making sure that as the units unfold, your students' work gets progressively better.

WHAT IF CHILDREN ENTER THIRD GRADE AS CAPABLE WRITERS BUT WITHOUT A BACKGROUND IN K–2 UNITS OF STUDY?

It is true that the third-grade units were devised with the expectation that children would enter third grade having already studied narrative, information, and opinion writing, with many children presumably studying these within the units that are captured in the second-grade books. But it is worth noting that the second-grade units extend and enrich the K–1 units in a fashion that is less meat-and-potatoes than the units in K–1 or in third grade. For example, in second grade there is a unit on lab reports and science information books and a unit on writing poetry. Both those units will take students' skills far, but their specific content isn't absolutely foundational to the third-grade series.

An Overview of the Expectations and Supports in the Third-Grade Units

There are four books that provide detailed support for third-grade units. Each of those units of study tends to last five or perhaps six weeks. The four units provide the crucial support that third-graders need to meet the CCSS. The instruction enables students to work in narrative, opinion, and information writing with increasing sophistication and with decreasing reliance on scaffolds. For example, while first-graders write Small Moment stories by recalling an event and retelling it "across their fingers," third-graders' plot narratives using the graphic organizer of a timeline or a story mountain, and revise the narratives so that beginnings and endings relate to what the story is really about. In a similar manner, in first grade, children make and substantiate claims in persuasive letters. By third grade, they learn to use expository structures to persuade.

The series provides maximum support for four units, and helps you design additional units on your own. This book specifically helps you design and teach units that supplement the units laid out in detail. While the unit books contain the minilessons, small-group work, conferring, and checklists that you need to teach those units, this book will provide only an overview, a path that you could take your class on if you undertake one of the units described here.

The third-grade year begins and ends with a focus on narrative writing (*Crafting True Stories* and *Once Upon a Time: Adapting and Writing Fairy Tales*). You will not question one unit on narrative writing—that is required by the Common Core State Standards—but you might question two narrative units. There are a number of reasons for this. First, we always support the three main types of writing, and then alternate the type of writing that receives an additional unit. In fourth grade, this emphasis goes to opinion writing, for example. Second, the level of narrative writing that the CCSS expect is especially high. Study the fourth-grade narrative writing sample, for example, in Appendix B of the Common Core State Standards document, contrasting it with the third-grade information writing sample about a horse, and you'll agree that your students won't reach the level of the narrative sample without more than one intensive unit a year on narrative writing. In general, the narrative texts in Appendix B (those that represent the CCSS' expectations) are far more sophisticated than texts in other genres. Then, too, an ability to write narratives well will allow students to embed narratives in all their writing, including anecdotes in essays, for example. Finally, it is during work with narrative writing that students learn to write with fluency, with a command of conventions, with detail, and with structure. Later, all these skills can be transferred to other genres.

The second book in the series, *The Art of Information Writing*, provides students with help writing information books on areas of personal expertise. This book conveys that information writing is really a form of writing to teach and channels students to design a course that they teach through writing. The table of contents is a big part of this unit, with students learning to chunk their information into chapters. They also learn a whole armload of ways to lift the level of their information writing including learning to write with bricks of information and to hold these together with the cement of ideas. Students proceed along, writing a sequence of chapters, and as they learn new qualities of effective information writing, they incorporate those new qualities into the chapter they are just about to write and also revise chapters they wrote earlier, thereby giving themselves a great deal of practice putting the new knowledge to work. As they proceed in this way, they also become much more experienced revisers.

The third book, *Changing the World: Persuasive Speeches, Petitions, and Editorials*, helps students write opinion writing of all kinds—persuasive speeches, petitions, persuasive letters, editorials—in the service of a cause. The students learn to organize opinion writing so that they are advancing a claim across a large swath of text, and they learn to use information and ideas, rhetoric, and voice to persuade. The unit emphasizes the importance of considering one's audience, angling information to be persuasive to the particular readers one has in mind.

The fourth book, *Once Upon a Time: Adapting and Writing Fairy Tales*, invites students to first write adaptations of a few familiar fairy tales and to eventually write their own original fairy tales. Leaning on the support of the original story, children learn to use literary language and storytelling prowess to create the world of the story and to write gripping stories that crescendo. Although children think this is a unit on fairy tales, teachers know they are teaching narrative craft. This is a highly motivating unit that asks the world of students yet provides enormous support, both by asking children to stay within the bearing walls of an existing story and by channeling them to use storytelling repeatedly throughout the process of writing.

DEVELOPING AN IF . . . THEN . . . CURRICULUM BASED ON YOUR CHILDREN'S NEEDS

Earlier, I discussed the fact that if children are writing like first- and second-graders, they don't just need a different unit for the start of the year; they need different tools and timetables. That can be provided by teaching the first alternative unit in this book, "Writing Gripping Fictional Stories with Meaning and Significance." Or, if you have access to the second-grade set of Units of Study books, you could teach *Lessons from the Masters: Improving Narrative*

Writing. A third option, if you have access to the earlier edition of the primary Units of Study for Primary Writing, is that you could teach a quick, ramped-up version of *Small Moments: Personal Narrative Writing*. Teaching any one of those options as a preliminary unit would help your children enter the first third-grade unit in strong stead.

"Writing Gripping Fictional Stories" could also set children up for success with the very challenging unit, *Once Upon a Time*. If you teach this unit toward the end of third grade, just prior to that unit, adjust the paper on which students write so these are full sheets of notebook paper, stapled into booklets, and expect more planning and rehearsal and revision up front, before students actually write a whole story.

Then again, most third-graders will absolutely be ready for *Crafting True Stories*, and in most instances, you'll want to teach that unit straightaway. In the thousands of classrooms in which we work most closely, we have often found that children can use a follow-up unit on narrative writing. The *Crafting True Stories* unit serves to induct students into the writing workshop, into writer's notebooks, into the third-grade version of the writing process, and they can come from that unit without yet producing the strongest stories in the world. If you find you are tempted to prolong that first unit until students' writing is better, we suggest instead that you add on a second narrative unit, and "Writing Gripping Fictional Stories" works very well in that case. Your students will be wildly enthusiastic for a unit in fiction writing, so it is hard to go wrong with the unit. There will be instances when you can ramp it up, because the unit was originally designed for second grade or for the start of third grade, but that is easy to accomplish.

Before you approach units in information and opinion writing, you will again do on-demand assessments to gauge whether your children are close to grade level when they enter these units. If they are not and you have access to the Units of Study books from second grade, you might borrow one of those books and teach that unit prior to the third-grade unit supporting the same type of writing. But we do not think that is necessary.

You may decide, however, that your students would benefit from more than one cycle through an information unit. After you teach *The Art of Information Writing*, you may want to teach a second, rather parallel unit, this time one that helps students to use writing as a tool to learn about a content area and then write as an extension of that unit. We've included "Information Writing: Reading, Research, and Writing in the Content Areas" and suggest you teach it any time after *The Art of Information Writing*. This could be months later.

"Poetry: Writing, Thinking, and Seeing More" ushers children into a study not just of poetry, but of reading and writing connections, and teaches writers to care about craft and its relation to meaning. By playing with language and craft, studying mentor texts, and revising, children will learn not only to write more effective poetry but also to care about craft and to read like writers. The CCSS' emphasis on close reading of complex texts and the focus on reading to notice authorial decisions make a unit on poetry especially appropriate.

Then, too, we have included a description of a rather challenging unit for third-graders, "The Literary Essay: Equipping Ourselves with the Tools to Write Expository Texts that Advance an Idea about Literature." This unit relies upon students already having learned about opinion writing in *Changing the World*. Now, instead of writing in support of recycling or more books in the school library, students write in support of ideas they have about very familiar texts. We imagine this as a short unit—three or four weeks in length—and as an entirely optional unit for third-graders who are on the strong side and need more enrichment.

At the end of third grade, you may choose to immerse your students in a revision study. The "Revision" unit in this book gives writers the opportunity to revisit and rewrite old pieces of writing, lifting the level of the work they did in given genres across the year. Revision can be a hard sell for writers of all ages and yet proves again and again to be one of the most powerful tools writers possess. This unit will go a long way toward helping your young writers jump on the revision bandwagon!

While the Units of Study series support units that vary according to grade level, it is also true that all of the units aim to teach writers the essentials of good writing, and those essentials are generally applicable across genres. Eudora Welty once said, "Poetry is the school I went to in order to learn to write prose." That is, work in any particular genre can advance writing skills that are applicable across genres. Interestingly, the essential skills of great writers remain consistent whether the writer is seven years old, seventeen, or seventy. All of us try again and again to write with focus, detail, grace, structure, clarity, insight, honesty, and increasing control of conventions, and all of us do so by rehearsing, planning, studying exemplar texts, drafting, rereading, revising, re-imagining, and editing.

Part One: Alternate and Additional Units

Writing Gripping Fictional Stories with Meaning and Significance

RATIONALE/INTRODUCTION

This unit has been a longtime favorite. Children will approach the unit with abundant ambition and zeal, ready to write, write, write. The invitation to write fiction leads to new volume, new stamina, and new engagement. Children's scrawl will fill one page, then another, one book and another, as the unit taps into a great source of energy.

You have choices about how you will spin the unit and about the skills you will emphasize. If the unit is being taught to students who have had units of study instruction prior to now, chances are that they'll approach this unit already knowing the essentials about writing Small Moment stories. They will know that it helps to zoom in on a particular scene—say, an event that occurs across fifteen minutes—and to write the story of that event in a step-by-step fashion so that readers can relive the event, picturing what the main character said and did first, then what occurred in response. If children have experienced units of study on narrative writing, they'll also approach this unit already knowing about the value of stretching out the most important parts of those stories.

On the other hand, if children have not studied writing through units of study in K–2, they may not have been taught what we regard as a crucial concept: that it is far easier to write an effective story if one zooms in on a small moment, a particular scene, and writes that small moment, that scene, as a storyteller might tell it, allowing readers to almost live in the shoes of the character. That is, a child who has not studied units of study in writing might approach the project of writing a story about a boy who learns to do a magic trick, planning to start the story, "Once upon a time a boy named Michael wanted to do a magic trick and so he did it. The audience cheered and he smiled big." Contrast that lead with "Michael held his deck of cards. He walked up to the stage and said, 'Good evening, ladies and gentlemen.'" You'll need, then, to be sure to highlight this part of your instruction. The unit contains lots of spaces for you to do that.

Either way, children come to this unit with a background not only as writers but also as readers. They've read narrative picture books and chapter books in which each chapter is rather like a self-contained story. Your children's experiences with short stories (whether in picture books, in episodic chapter books, or in collections of short stories) provides them with a reservoir to draw upon. It will be important for them to understand that they are being asked to write in ways that re-create the sounds and rhythms of stories. As you help children draw on their knowledge as readers, keep in mind that you are supporting their abilities to talk and think about published texts and about authors' craft in those texts. This is highly supportive of CCSS reading standards 4, 5, and 6.

This unit prioritizes story structure, spotlighting the plotting work that a short story writer does, emphasizing especially that a good story contains a scene (or small moment) or two and is told to build gripping tension. The character wants something and encounters trouble en route to that something. For your children, you capture this combination of motivations and obstacles by characterizing the stories they'll be writing as "edge-of-the-seat stories" or "trouble stories." That is, this is not just about a character who does something—performs a magic trick in front of an audience—but it is about a character who wants something, who encounters trouble. The story comes not from performing the magic trick, but from wanting to do well and struggling to master the trick. Tension can turn a sequential chain of events into something that feels like a story. To do this, teach your students how to develop characters in a way that builds tension, giving them dreams, desires, fears, and frustrations.

One big goal of this unit (and any writing unit) is to help children write with volume. Meanwhile, you will also aim to raise the quality of your children's narrative writing, bearing in mind that the ultimate goal is for children to write well-elaborated short stories.

Before you begin this unit, think back to when you were about eight years old. Chances are, you recall a story or two you wrote or wanted to write. Was there a character in that story who had a giant feeling weltering inside of her or him? Did that character want something—a friend, a prize, a chance—so badly it hurt? These are the feelings your children have surely had, and their characters can have these feelings too. Teach kids that in good fiction, characters' wants, hopes, and aches are big. Then give your students space to write—and let their imaginations run free.

A SUMMARY OF THE BENDS IN THE ROAD FOR THIS UNIT

In Bend I (Think of a Character and of Small Moment Stories for that Character: Generating and Writing Several Short Fiction Books), you will set children up to generate a bunch of Small Moment, edge-of-the-seat story ideas and then quickly choose one and get started, first storytelling it to a partner before sitting down to write, write, write. Children will write several focused stories during this first bend, writing in booklets. You will teach strategies on storytelling focused Small Moment scenes rather than summarizing, on using detail to build tension, and on stretching out the most gripping parts. Plan to spend at least a week in this bend. If children have never been in a Small Moment unit of study, this will require at least a week and a half.

In Bend II (Revise with Intention: Pull Readers to the Edges of Their Seats), children will return to the stories they have written, revising these stories for greater meaning and tension. They may revise by writing whole new versions of their stories, reaching toward the goal of storytelling rather than summarizing. If they have written their stories in a such a way that the drama unfolds on the pages, then their revision will mostly involve reworking their drafting booklets, revising like carpenters. They'll add pages and flaps and extenders to their booklets as they learn how to stretch out the "heart" of the story (the part that gets readers gripping their seats in anticipation), how to complicate the problem, and how to also build tension by having the character attempt first one thing, then another, and then another to solve the problem before finding a way to resolve things. In short, children will learn how to revise with intention. If this unit comes at the start of the third-grade year, you'll want to keep it short, so we suggest you allow about a week to make your way through Bend II. If this is more of an enrichment unit, coming midway in the third-grade year, you can decide whether this bend provides a lot of extension opportunities (we think it can) and extend it to two weeks if you like.

In Bend III (Repeat the Process and Accumulate Lessons Along the Way), children will repeat the process, this time focusing on doing all that they can do to make their stories even better. Children will self-assess at the start of and throughout this bend, setting goals for themselves based on the narrative checklist, on charts around the room, and on what they see in their writing. To support this push toward writing the best stories possible, you may teach them strategies to be sure that the parts of their stories fit together or teach them to write more compelling endings, perhaps ones that convey a message to readers. Bend III could also take a week and a half. Expect students to produce at least three stories (two in each week, or more if this bend is longer than that).

GETTING READY
Gather Texts for Students

As with all units of study, you will want to select mentor texts to accompany your teaching so that you can provide your writers with examples. Some gripping picture books we recommend using throughout this unit are *Shortcut*, by Donald Crews; *Too Many Tamales*, by Gary Soto; *Koala Lou*, by Mem Fox; and *The Ghost-Eye Tree*, by Bill Martin. Or you might use parts of an early-reader chapter book from a series (Kate DiCamillo's Mercy Watson, James Howe's Pinky and Rex, Barbara Park's Junie B. Jones, or Suzy Kline's Horrible Harry are some possibilities). And remember that you have stories from your life that you can write with meaning, significance, and tension as a way to demonstrate for your children all that is possible. You can tailor these pieces of writing to demonstrate the skills your students need.

Use Additional Resources as Needed

You will also want to consult books on children's literature because any such book can teach you the language that fiction writers use to describe their craft, and that language can lift your teaching in this unit. Of course, it is always important to draw on the work of the children in your classroom. Workshop teaching is most powerful when you respond and teach to your kids' successes and struggles. In the end, a good portion of your teaching will revolve around the responsive instruction you provide as you move kids along trajectories of skill development. You'll want to become accustomed to fine-tuning your teaching through an attentiveness to student work, because the work your students do is not just showing you what they can or can't do; it is also showing you what *you* can do.

Choose When and How Children Will Publish

Your students are likely to generate many pieces of writing during this unit. During the second and third bends you will emphasize revision, and students will have the opportunity to deeply revise a book from the first bend and another book from the third bend. Those final stories can all be published in some fashion. For the publishing celebration, however, children will presumably need to choose just one of these stories to share; perhaps it will be one that builds the most tension or carries the most significance. Just as the gripping stories you read aloud to your class are meant to be discussed, so too are the gripping stories your students will write worthy of discussion. You may want to model your celebration after your whole-class read-aloud, giving students an opportunity to read their stories aloud and then giving listeners a chance to have a discussion. That, of course, would need to happen in small groups. You might do this with just your class or perhaps invite outsiders to participate in the celebration.

BEND I: THINK OF A CHARACTER AND OF SMALL MOMENT STORIES FOR THAT CHARACTER: GENERATING AND WRITING SEVERAL SHORT FICTION BOOKS

Introduce the genre.

Your students will undoubtedly be eager to write fiction, especially because they will by now be avid readers of fiction. Throughout this unit, the most important message you'll convey is this: writers use everything they know to make up their own stories. You'll tell your children, "You can write realistic fiction stories about a character you dream up." That is, you will want to make it clear to your children that they will be writing realistic fiction stories. If you are teaching this unit after *Crafting True Stories*, you will encourage writers to draw on all the craft moves they learned from studying mentor authors in that unit and all the strategies they now hold in their repertoire for writing small moments. The Common Core State Standards call for third-graders to write sequenced narratives, in which they establish the situation and introduce the narrator or characters, and provide a sense of closure. So, you will want to help your writers think about the arc and language of their stories, about the passage of time, and about the need for a conclusion that brings the story together. The goal for this unit will be to write well-elaborated short stories.

Announce with some fanfare: "Writers, you have an exciting opportunity ahead of you. You are going to write edge-of-the-seat *fiction* stories. This means that you'll write stories that keep your readers wanting more, ones that make them think, 'Oh no, how will this story end?' and 'Oh my goodness, I can't wait to turn the page.' Edge-of-the-seat fiction stories are exactly what you think they are: fiction stories that put readers, literally, on the edges of their seats!"

You might then read an example of a story that is fictional, but realistic, and keeps readers on the edges of their seats. As mentioned earlier, *Shortcut*, by Donald Crews; *The Ghost-Eye Tree*, by Bill Martin; *Koala Lou*, by Mem Fox; and *Too Many Tamales*, by Gary Soto, are four great examples, and they represent a range of ways to build tension. Some teachers share tension-filled clips from movies, such as the garbage incinerator scene from *Toy Story 3*. If you elect to do that, you can narrate and story-tell as the scene unfolds to show children how a writer builds tension.

Meanwhile teach students to generate focused story ideas and choose between them.

While you introduce the genre, you'll also take the first day or two of the unit to teach children a few strategies to generate Small Moment fictional stories—fictional episodes—in which a character encounters trouble and somehow resolves it. Children will not need more than two strategies for generating gripping stories, but they will use those strategies often because they'll probably generate a handful of possible ideas, then choose and write one story, and then they'll generate another handful of ideas and choose and write another story.

Both of the strategies that we most suggest involve students thinking of a strong emotion, one that they feel sometimes and one that characters in the books they read also sometimes feel. The writer might select jealousy, embarrassment, frustration, surprise, or hope. And both of the strategies the writer making up a character and thinking of Small Moment stories (or "one time whens") involve that character had one of those feelings.

One strategy for generating fictional stories begins with young writers thinking of "one time whens" from books that they have read. A child might think, for example, of the awful embarrassment Pinky felt when he wet his pants during the spelling bee (in *Pinky and Rex and the Spelling Bee*). Then the job is to create a similar moment for a fictional character. Maybe the child who began by thinking about Pinky's embarrassing moment might make up a story in which a character trips on the stage during a piano recital or forgets her lines during the school play or misses the ball during tryouts for the softball team. Another child, who began by thinking of how desperately Ramona wants to pull her rival Susan Kushner's long blonde curls—and the moment when she does—might imagine his or her character is jealous of someone and longs to bring that person down in some way. Imagine the tension-filled scene leading up to the character realizing this dream. The idea is to create a fictional character, zoom in on a strong emotion, and then create a time when that fictional character experienced that strong emotion.

Children's literature is full of characters who ache and want and worry and fume, so it won't be hard for your students to find an emotion or a scenario they can latch onto as a template they can borrow to help them with the story of their own making. Suspenseful fiction is full of stories of characters wanting something out of reach, not fitting in, getting into trouble, embarrassing themselves, and facing danger. Your children can draw on these topics and spin them in their own unique way.

Another strategy for coming up with an idea for a fictional story involves starting with small moments from one's own life instead of from literature. These stories can then be fictionalized or told from a different perspective to bring out the tension. For example, perhaps a student thinks of a moment when she was lost in the grocery store. In reality, she was only apart from her family for a minute or so, but in a realistic fiction story, the character might be lost for an entire day and maybe not in a grocery store but on the city streets. Often students will find that telling realistic stories based on real life is a powerful way to show how an event really felt. Sometimes the actual facts don't convey the powerful emotions that surround the moments from life that really matter.

Whichever strategy you teach and your children use, be sure that generating a list of possible realistic fiction ideas takes children ten minutes, not the entire workshop time, and that they then pick one to start writing about. Some teachers suggest that children generate something like four story ideas, then write the first page of a few of those stories, and then choose one to write as a whole story, leaving the remaining first pages as books-in-waiting.

As children plan stories, steer them to write with focus, limiting their characters and scope, and to plan through storytelling before drafting.

Your goal in this unit is for children to write stories that comprise two small moments (or scenes) at most, so this means that it is essential that you guide your kids to select story ideas that can happen in one or two twenty-minute stretches of time. Make sure that many of the stories you study as mentor texts during this unit also cover short periods of time (picture books or short chapter books tend to work best for this) so that children have models. Likewise, children should focus on maybe one or two realistic characters rather than a large cast, and the main character should be close in age to the writer. This will allow the writer to get into the head of that character and to develop all the characters with some essential details rather than presenting them superficially one after another on the page.

One of the ways to channel children toward stories that are limited in scope and follow a clear arc is to continually remind them of all they know about Small Moment personal narrative writing. Make sure you remind them that instead of writing "watermelon stories" in which they tell all about their character's life or time at camp, they are writing about a single seed story. Ask, "If you are writing about a character who went shopping at the mall and got lost, will you start when the character walks into the mall? When the character's mother says, 'I'll be right back?' Or when?"

Take time at the start of the unit to help children practice telling their stories aloud, telling their stories across pages of a drafting booklet a few times, first to themselves and then to their writing partners or to you during a conference or to the whole class during shares. As students improve their stories with each verbal retelling, make sure they have a system for quickly jotting down their ideas. For instance, they can sketch a quick, tiny picture in the top corner of each page to help them remember their plans. After they have story-told and planned their stories in their drafting booklets (which should take fifteen minutes, not days!) they need to draft. They'll need five- to seven-page booklets in which to write, with each page of the booklet essentially functioning like one more dot on the timeline of the event. Imagine that it should take children no more than a day and a half to write the whole story, front to finish. We have found that if children prolong this process for too long, the stories become disjointed.

Encourage volume in both quantity of stories generated and depth of individual stories.

If some children get going strong, they may ask if they can staple more pages onto their booklets. We suggest that instead of encouraging sprawling, long stories, you channel your children's fervor for fiction into writing one fictional story after another. This also means that you'll want to teach students that "when you're done, you've just begun." When a story is completed, it can be stored on one side of the writing folder and their unfinished stories on the other side of the folder. After completing one story, the writer can then go back to choose another idea from a list generated earlier, or make a new list of story ideas, and complete the process again. There should never be a reason to be completely stuck. If a story has become difficult, the writer can store it in the folder and work on something else. From time to time you might remind students to reread all the stories in their folders to see whether there is more they might add to them. Children love to tell a good story—the kind that gets a reaction. Take this energy and use it to stretch their volume of writing. Expect most children to write two or three stories per week. Some might write two or three stories during the entire unit but these will be children who write several completely new drafts per week. Either way, you will expect the volume to continually increase.

Depending on the needs of your students and when you choose to teach this unit, writers may be working on loose-leaf paper or in booklets. If you begin with them writing in booklets, similar to the way of writing that you expect to see second graders do, as the unit progresses, you may push them to write more. You might say, "Writers, over the past few days I have noticed you going through more booklets than ever before. You are filling your five-page booklets and then picking up another one and beginning the next story. I'm thinking that instead of moving on to the next story, you might want to try to stretch one story. Before, you used to write in five-page booklets that had half a dozen lines on each page, but now I see that you are ready to stretch your writing over more pages with more lines. You will write just as much as before, but this time instead of writing a few different stories, you are going to go deeper into one story, adding more and stretching it out to show the importance of it."

Have students use writing partners to help them elaborate with focus.

We hope that when presented with the added space, children's eyes will light up and their hands will begin to move faster than ever before. However, sometimes, children meet the business of writing longer stories with groans and complaints. Not surprisingly, the single most powerful ingredient in children's enthusiasm is your enthusiasm and attitude. If you focus too much on volume, demanding that students write a minimum number of pages, it is likely that students will bend their heads faithfully to this task, creating a minimum number of pages that will be just that: minimum. Instead, if you present the opportunity to write longer stories as a new freedom or even as a characteristic of more accomplished writers, your young writers are more likely to be so excited by the challenge to fill the space that they will begin to write as much as possible across those pages. You might show how, as a writer comes to know more about how to craft a story, she simply needs more space to tell the story with all the details that help the story come alive for the reader. One teacher we know used a well-loved picture book and wrote an alternative version with only half the text, saying that the author might have chosen to write her story this way. She presented this bare-bones version to students, who easily recognized that the shorter story had lost much of its significance and power compared with the original. The same effect might be achieved using your own model text or the story of a shared class experience.

The challenge, of course, will be to help students write more while staying within two short episodes. You do not want your students to elongate their stories by including extraneous details or writing "bed to bed" stories (a story that begins when the main character wakes up in bed in the morning and ends when the character goes to bed at night). Rather, you will want to help them keep their focus on a short snippet of their characters' lives, zooming in to elaborate with details that add tension. Help students stretch out the action in their episodes, going bit by bit through each small moment. For example, instead of writing, "I opened the door," a child might write, "I gripped the knob and pulled with all my might."

One strategy for helping students figure out how to say more is to encourage them to share their story with their writing partner and to check whether their story is having the effect they hoped for. A writer might read the first portion of his story aloud and then ask, "What are you picturing?" or "Does that part make sense?" Feedback such as, "I'm confused. Can you say more? What do you really mean?" can help writers to add more and more to their stories to clarify and extend. Their pages will become filled, and the need for more lines and extra pages will become clear.

To practice visualizing how each bit of the story went, partners could act out their stories for each other. They can go page by page, acting out what happened and then quickly writing down all the things they did. So the writer working on stretching out the part where he opens the door might stand up and act out opening a door with his partner. Then, the two can sit down and write all the little things that the writer had to do to get that door open.

BEND II: REVISE WITH INTENTION: PULL READERS TO THE EDGES OF THEIR SEATS

Teach students to make their stories come alive by storytelling with detail and thinking about the internal journey of their characters.

In this bend in the road of the unit, the focus shifts from drafting to revision, from writing with volume to writing effective stories. Your goal now is to dramatically improve your students' writing so that their stories come alive and brim with meaning. Toward this end, one important focus will be storytelling with detail, not summarizing. Teach children that to tell a story, a writer first decides what the story is about: "This is a story about a girl who wants a dog because all her friends have one. At first her parents say no, but eventually, after a struggle, she gets it." Next, the writer envisions each small moment of the story, rather than storytelling the whole of the story, which often leads children to summarize. ("Emily wanted a dog. 'Can I have one?' she asked. Her mother said, 'No,' because they didn't have the money. Then one day she was walking to school and she saw something and it was a dog. The end.")

Teach children to ask themselves, "What, exactly, will happen at the start of my story?" The writer of the story about a girl who longs for a dog might think, "If the girl wants a dog, what can I have her do that shows this? If this were a play, what would she be doing on stage?" Perhaps the main character talks to her mother about getting a dog. The child might write, "Emily walked into the kitchen. Her mom was making dinner. 'Mom! Mom! Can I have a dog? Annie has one and it's really cute,' Emily whined." Or the writer might create an opening moment in which Emily gazes longingly at her friend's dog. Finally, teach children to make movies in their minds of the exact story, imagining it bit by bit as they write.

Reliving stories, imagining the events unfolding, elicits writing that is organized and fluid. Children often write sequenced stories with greater elaboration. One of the best ways to help children imagine a story is by acting it out. As children act out one moment and then another, they can not only record what each character says and does but also describe each bit of the story in detail, including where the characters are and what is happening around them. Partners can work together to find words that describe the actions and bring voice to the dialogue they act out together. Children can also look closely at the books they are reading to explore how those authors bring their favorite characters to life. Teach them how to study those texts to discover ways authors use time transitions to make each scene of their story flow. This will help children transition more smoothly from one part of the story to the next and also use more sophisticated sentence structures as they compose their own stories.

As your students story-tell and act out parts of their stories, they'll then turn to their drafts and make changes so that their written work matches their oral rehearsal. In the first bend you taught children that they could story-tell across the pages to figure out how the story might go and then make a quick sketch in the top corner of each page. In this bend, you might build on that strategy, teaching kids that they can sketch to plan what happens but also to plan how the character will feel on each page of the story. They can do this by either jotting a word or two along with the sketch or matching the faces of the characters to the feelings conveyed. You can share with kids that one of the many secrets to good fiction writing is that writers pay attention to what's happening on both the outside of the character and the inside. On the outside a character might be walking down the street, carrying a backpack. On the inside, he's thinking, "I'm so nervous! I hope the other kids will like me!" As kids develop plans for new stories, they can begin to think about the internal journey of their characters (their thoughts, feelings, worries, struggles), as well as the external journey.

Children might also look to their favorite books and characters to see how good writers flesh out their characters in ways that bring them to life, showing their feelings rather than telling them. You might say, "To write stories that will draw readers in, you can look at the work of other writers who have done this, noticing how they show to bring their characters to life." "Emily walked into the kitchen where her mother stood cooking dinner. She said, 'Mom, I'm the only kid at school without a dog!' Emily felt hopeful. She stood, eyes wide, fingers crossed, holding her breath." Notice how this example weaves dialogue with characters' actions and thoughts and feelings. Teach your children to do likewise. It is through a combination of these details that characters come to life. If you are teaching this unit after *Crafting True Stories*, you can similarly remind children that when they revise fiction, they can draw on the exact same techniques they used for revision of personal narratives. Keep your charts that support elaboration and revision from this previous unit front and center.

Teach students to create tension by including obstacles, complicating problems, and challenging situations.

Another important focus of this bend, of course, will be on building tension. Reiterate to your students that tension is that quality in a story that compels the reader to keep turning the pages out of eagerness to know what happens next. Tension keeps the reader on the edge of his seat! Writers weave tension throughout the story, especially at the beginning. Tension builds the momentum of the story. Early in a story, it can help to include a line or two that shows how the character is feeling or what she is thinking. This shows the inner story and piques the curiosity of readers, encouraging them to read on, anticipating what will happen next. You might say to children, "You know how when you read, you often think, 'I bet such-and-such will happen next!' You want the readers of your stories to think like that too, but they need your help. They need you to drop a hint here or there so that they can begin to guess what might happen next. You can do this by sharing what a character is thinking or feeling."

The easiest way to create tension is to make it hard for the main character to get what he or she wants. In a story about a girl who wants desperately to visit her grandmother in South America, the writer should create a situation that keeps her from getting on that plane. The writer might ask herself, "What will make this difficult to achieve? Does the girl's father not want her to go? Is the girl afraid of flying? Is the plane ticket too expensive?" Encourage your writers to ask, "What trouble will get in my character's way—stop him from getting what he wants?"

Extra paper can also help with tension. Teach young writers to insert entire pages into the important parts of their stories to make sure they are telling those parts bit by bit, drawing them out. You are keeping them from just adding more pages at the end. This is revision with a purpose, as opposed to revision merely for the sake of revision.

Teach writers that as the story continues, they can add more hurdles that make things hard for the main character, and that leaves the reader thinking, "What is going to happen next?" You might teach kids that often there are several "bumps in the road." If you are modeling a story about the time two friends went bike riding and one had an accident, you might begin with the moment when one friend fell off her bike. Then, in the next part of your story, perhaps the other character notices that her friend has cut her upper lip and is bleeding. She tries to help her up to walk back home when she realizes that her friend has sprained her ankle and can't move. Now the problem spirals from a fall off the bike into a major accident, leaving the reader thinking, "Oh, no! How are they going to get out of this?"

BEND III: REPEAT THE PROCESS AND ACCUMULATE LESSONS ALONG THE WAY

Have students reflect on past work and set goals for future work.

You can help children assess their writing using the Narrative Writing checklist. They can evaluate their writing, deciding whether it includes the skills on the learning progression, and if not, decide what they need to do to make sure that it does. You may also ask them to look for evidence of one or two additional skills that you have taught.

These concepts are sophisticated for young writers, so you will want children to practice them in lots of pieces. Each time they begin a new five-page booklet or draft, encourage them to draw on all that they have learned so far, aiming to make their next book even better. You might say to children that the first thing any writer must do before beginning a new story is to sit down and think about what she knows makes for good writing. Then the writer sets a plan for what she will do to improve her writing. When writers embark on new stories, they need to ask themselves, "What did I do in my last story that made it so good I want to do it again? What else might I try?" And if your children are returning to a piece they began the day before, they might look at it and ask, "What else might I work on today to make this my strongest piece of writing yet?" To support this work during your conferences, you will want to refer to the charts and to their plans. You might ask, "What is your plan for today? What goal are you working on as a writer?" Then you will likely want to help your students set up plans of action for carrying out their self-selected goals.

Teach students to revise for elaboration and character by storytelling to uncover important details and adding dialogue to highlight important character traits.

Plan to spend the first portion of this final bend encouraging children to use all they know to write lots of stories, and then plan to spend the final portion of this bend emphasizing revision. Revision, you'll remind them, is a complement to good writing. If they have a small stack of stories that they like, those stories merit being revised. If a child really doesn't like one or two of the books she has written, those texts might not warrant revision.

Take this time to encourage students to study anchor charts and think, "What will I work on today? How will I make my piece the very, very best it can be?" Then, with their plans in mind, they can gather the necessary materials from the classroom writing center before diving into their work. Of course, to facilitate this work, you will need to ensure that children have access to the necessary materials. You will likely want to provide them with a revision folder and a colored pen, swatches of paper on which they can add paragraphs to their drafts, and flaps of paper that can be taped over parts of the story they decide to revise. Teach them to use staple removers, if they don't already use these regularly, so they can make their books longer or shorter.

Because it is likely that many children are still summarizing rather than storytelling with detail, you can expect that one of the most important reasons for third-graders to revise will be to elaborate. If a child wrote, "For Jorge's birthday, he got a bike," teach this child that he can cross out that summary of the event and instead story-tell exactly what happened, step by step. Be aware that injunctions to "add more information" or "add details" don't necessarily help writers to shift from summarizing to storytelling. Instead, such comments too often lead to pages that contain a lot of summary—pages like this: "For Jorge's birthday, he got a bike. It was red and had a basket. He liked it. He was happy. It was a great, great bike." So coach children to make a movie in their mind, to think, "What did the character say or do exactly?" and to tell the story bit by bit. For example, instead of writing "Jorge got a bike," the writer might write, "The box was really big. Jorge closed his eyes and wished. 'Please, please, please let it be a bike,' he thought. 'Go on, open it,' his dad said. Jorge pulled back the top and saw a red thing. Could it be? Then there was a basket. 'A bike!' Jorge yelled. He was happy."

All students can do the same sort of revision with any story. Help them check to be sure they are storytelling, creating little scenes in their minds using dialogue and small actions to let the story unfold on the page.

If you are teaching this unit as an enrichment unit for strong third-graders, you might teach your students that writers of fiction often use dialogue not just to show what's happening but also to show characters' personalities. Since you can make characters say anything, why not have them say things that show what they are like? A bully wouldn't just say, "Pass me the peas, please." She might instead say something like, "Hey, Stupid, hand over the peas!" In a minilesson, you might demonstrate how you reread your writing, revision pen in hand, focusing just on the dialogue and saying to yourself, "Is there something else this character could say that would show his personality?" To help figure out what the character could say and do, you might suggest that kids think of a person in real life who is like the character they are trying to create and imagine what that real person might say. They could also think of a familiar character from a book or a movie.

Have students revise for meaning.

You might also teach children that it can help to think about the really important life lessons their character learns and to show those life lessons. Often a writer will add something about those lessons as a way to end a story. "From that day on, Anna always remembered that she could take the time to make her grandma happy." Or, "After that, Otto always remembered to keep his toys in his backpack until recess time, and he didn't get in trouble again."

Channel students to try out literary leads and endings that send a message.

You might also teach children to create more literary beginnings or endings. It is useful to show kids that they can try writing a few different versions of a lead or an ending (or any part of their story, for that matter) before deciding which one works best. To broaden their understanding of the various ways published story beginnings and endings are structured, children could study mentor texts the class has read, trying to name what the writer did in his or her beginning or ending.

As mentioned earlier, you may decide to make endings a big deal. The Common Core State Standards for reading call for children to be able to recount stories and determine their central message or lesson, as well as explain how it is conveyed by key details in the text, by the end of third grade. You might ask your children to do this same kind of lesson or message work in their writing. Teach children to ask themselves, "What does my story teach other people?" Kids might do this work with a partner. The partners might read each other's writing and then try to jot down what the main character learned—or what they learned. You may want to teach some of your more advanced writers that the lesson and the heart of the story usually go together. You could refer to the incinerator scene in *Toy Story 3* to help teach this concept. This scene sends the message that friends stick together no matter what.

Have students polish for publication.

As you near the end of this unit, tell children that they will be celebrating soon. To prepare, they should spend some time polishing their writing—capitalizing proper nouns such as names and special places, rereading to ensure the story remains in a third-person voice, and adding words or punctuation that may have been left out.

CELEBRATE STUDENT WRITING BY READING ALOUD AND HAVING BOOK TALKS

Your children will write many pieces during this unit, and you will likely have each child pick one that he or she will publish. Encourage students to reread their pieces to find the one that builds the most tension and/or carries the most significance. Then you might make your celebration an "accountable talk" celebration. Ask your authors to read their stories aloud to the class and then give the class time to talk about these moments. If you have done the message work described in the final bend above, you will be acknowledging especially that their stories are very important. They are so significant, they need to be read and also discussed. In preparation for this, children might practice reading these stories in their best read-aloud voices, slowing down at parts and then reading with excitement at others.

Alternatively, you might set up a time to share the stories with another class or older buddies in another grade. You might even add their stories to your classroom library to be shared year after year. (Your kids could group together the ones with similar messages.) Or each child could think of a place in the classroom or the school where his or her story might live. For example, stories about getting hurt might live in the nurse's office, or stories about being a new kid at a new school might live in the main office.

Whatever you choose to do with the writing from this unit, your larger message will be that you and your students have worked hard to make this writing stand shoulder to shoulder with the best writing on your classroom's and the school library's bookshelves. Perhaps you'll ask partners to work together, writing blurbs for the back of each other's books to convince people to read them.

Information Writing
Reading, Research, and Writing in the Content Areas

RATIONALE/INTRODUCTION

Writing is given a preeminent place as one of the "basics"—reading, 'ritin', and 'rithmitic—because it is a skill that enables learning across every discipline. It's important, then, that writing is linked to the social studies, science, math, and reading curriculums. This unit has been designed to allow teachers to actually bring discipline-based writing into the writing workshop. Students are asked to write about a content area they've been studying at another time of the day (during reading and/or science or social studies time). During writing, teachers help with the specific writing challenges that this discipline-based work poses (while also helping students grasp the subject matter). This unit, then, is an extension of the information writing unit, one that makes more space for research and text citation—skills that are important in the Common Core State Standards.

Third-graders will be asked to build on their knowledge of information writing and also their knowledge of how to use mentor texts to raise the quality of their writing. They will create nonfiction books on a topic that the class has studied.

A word about nonfiction texts. If you look at many of the nonfiction books that students read, you'll see that typically an information text is chunked into different sections, each addressing different subtopics. And often, most of those sections will be structured in a fashion that mirrors the structure of the whole information book, with different subheadings, each addressing a different subtopic. But some sections of a book are narratives or opinion writing or how-to writing. That is, most information writing is actually a composite text, containing subordinate sections that are organized according to the purpose and content of that section. The writing that students do in this unit, then, will end up containing some chapters that are not organized in subsections, but are instead narratives, how-tos, letters, lists, and opinions. Their finished books will look like the DK Readers or the Rosen Primary Source books.

As you lead this unit, remember that the Common Core State Standards expectations for third grade (and far more so for fourth grade) in information writing ask for a focus on structure and elaboration. You will recall that according to the CCSS, third-grade information writers should group related information (W.3.2), an expectation that seems to us to require organizational structures such as sections within a piece. It is worth noting that next year, in fourth grade, your writers will also be required to group related information within their *opinion writing*. Because they are not expected to group related information in opinion writing *this* year but *are* expected to in information writing, it's clear that the CCSS believe that learning this skill first in information writing will help writers transfer the work more easily. Thus, your students must leave this year understanding how and being able to do this work so that they are ready to transfer this skill to a new genre next year. Additionally, the CCSS expects third-grade writers to move toward a cohesive structure through the use of linking words and phrases as a way to connect information within sections (e.g., *also*, *another*, *and*, *more*, *but*), to introduce their topics, and to provide a sense of conclusion at the end.

A second important quality of informational writing, as you will recall, is elaboration. The CCSS state that third-grade writers should be able to develop topics with facts, definitions, and details, as well as illustrations when these are appropriate. We believe that it is important for informational writers to draw on a wealth of specific information. In addition to what is highlighted by the CCSS, this could include answers to questions, statistics, definitions, facts, terms, descriptions, observations, patterns, sequences, true anecdotes, and so on.

None of this will be new to students who have already experienced the unit *The Art of Information Writing*. This unit, then, can provide students with the opportunity for the additional practice they need to master the skills expected of them, and it can also give you an opportunity to teach toward independence. You will also want to use this as an assessment-based unit, one that allows you to shore up any skills that have yet to be developed.

A SUMMARY OF THE BENDS IN THE ROAD FOR THIS UNIT

In Bend I (Writing to Develop Expertise and Grow Ideas), children will write to learn. They will collect fodder by learning from videos, reading, and observations. They will write about new knowledge they have gleaned on the whole-class discipline-based topic. Students will learn to use observational writing, annotated timelines, embellished notes, and writing-to-grow-ideas as methods for recording their knowledge, reflecting on that knowledge, and growing ideas. Outside of writing time, children will be reading to learn, expanding their knowledge on the topic. It should take five to six days to get through Bend I.

In Bend II (Planning a Table of Contents and Writing Chapters [and meanwhile, sometimes returning to research]), students will select a subtopic of interest, plan a table of contents related to that subtopic, and begin writing chapters. Students will also practice using boxes and bullets as well as compare-and-contrast structures. They will work on grouping related information, using linking words between ideas and bits of information. As needed, students will cycle back to research, finding the information and developing the knowledge they need, although ideally most of the reading and research will occur outside the writing workshop. Plan to spend about a week in this bend.

In Bend III (Using Mentor Texts to Help Writers Revise Chapters They've Written and to Lift the Level of Upcoming Chapters), students will revise chapters they have already written and lift the level of upcoming writing. They will do this by studying mentor texts, articulating qualities of good writing, using the information checklist, and in general, being critical of their first-draft efforts and purposeful toward the goal of improving their writing. Students will revise with support from their mentor texts. Bend III should last five to seven days.

In Bend IV (Editing and Publishing to Get Ready to Teach Others), students will prepare to publish. They'll try their book out with readers, listening to their questions and learning what they take away from the book, which will lead to more audience-centered revisions. Students will also work to make sure that the layout and design and use of visuals in their texts supports the main ideas that they are trying to convey. Students will assess their writing one last time and use the checklist to guide them toward final improvements. For example, if they hadn't realized this prior to now, students will realize that information books typically include a conclusion. (The CCSS suggest that third-grade information writers include a concluding section.) It should take about three days to prepare for publication and to celebrate.

GETTING READY
Gather Texts for Students

The most important way to prepare for this unit is to develop expertise in students, to build up their knowledge, so they can write about a discipline-based subject in the writing workshop. The content you choose as the topic for their writing should be highly engaging. You'll want to choose a topic for which you have many, many resources: books, videos, primary documents. You'll want to be sure your whole class can study many subtopics within the main topic, so you'll ask yourself, "Does this topic have breadth?"

A country study lends itself very well to this kind of work—with the whole class researching and writing about a shared country—as long as when the time comes for students to focus on a subtopic, you expect third-graders' to choose an aspect of the country that interests them. Some children might write about music and famous musicians. Some might write about important historical events. Some might write about daily life in the country; some might write about education or the climate, flora, and fauna.

Whatever topic you choose, flood your children with images, facts, and stories about the content under study—doing that during reading time or social studies and science time, Even better, begin the work of studying the unit a week or two before launching this writing unit so children will begin on Day One with lots and lots to say. As your researchers become experts, they'll be eager to share what they've learned, as well as the ideas they have about all the new information they know.

Besides immersing your class in the content area that they will be writing in, it will be important that you also immerse them in the genre of information writing. Some of the books that they are using as content resources may also serve this purpose. However, do not let yourself be restricted to only content area information books. Feel free to go back to the mentor texts you used in *The Art of Information Writing* unit, and pull in new resources, such as books from the DK Readers or the Rosen Primary Source books.

Choose When and How Students Will Publish

The unit will culminate with a celebration in which the children teach about what they've learned to others from another grade level or another class in their grade. If the students in one class studied one topic, such as one country, and the students in another class studied a similar but different topic, such as a second country, the publication celebration might create an opportunity for compare and contrast work that is very much a part of the third-grade CCSS expectations.

Mandates, Tests, Standards

Before the unit starts you'll want to give your students an assessment to study how well they write informational texts. Use the on-demand assessment in informational writing. You will then want to tailor your teaching to the data you gather from this assessment. Your teaching needs to begin where your students are. If your students demonstrate (in the on-demand) that they have mastered some of the big work of the third-grade Common Core State Standards (such as introducing a topic clearly, separating it into subtopics, and organizing their writing in separate pages so that appropriate information is grouped together inside of these subtopics), then you may want to bump up the level of the work. If, on the other hand, your third-graders seem to still need support in mastering expectations of second-grade work, you can study the second-grade information checklist to remind you of some of the lessons students will need you to teach.

BEND I: WRITING TO DEVELOP EXPERTISE AND GROW IDEAS
Decide where students will be doing their research writing.

Before your dive into this unit, there are some decisions that you will need to make. You will want to decide where students will collect the notes and information that they'll need. Do you imagine the writer's notebooks as their place for note-taking on, say, Europe? Or their social studies notebooks? Might the students create special folders for this?

Decide, too, whether you want to channel children to research subtopics right away or whether that will wait for a few days into the unit. If you do want them to tackle subtopics, do you see those as individually "owned," or might you organize interest-based subtopics? For example, if you are choosing to study the European Community as a whole-class topic, you might steer the class into groups that study countries (or aspects of countries) within the European Community. You could also have children choose one of the social studies thematic strands as a lens through which to study a country or even compare and contrast more than one country. Examples of such lenses are culture; time, continuity, and change; people, places, and environments; individual development and identity; individuals, groups, and institutions; power, authority, and governance; production, distribution, and consumption; science, technology, and society; global connections; and civic ideas and responsibility. Of course, you would need to present these in ways that will be attractive to your third-graders. Children could also choose their own topics, choosing ones that come from their reading.

Teach students to use their notebooks as places to gather information about their topics. Methods to capture what they are learning include observational writing, sketching, boxes-and-bullets format, and questioning.

As the unit begins, you will immerse your children in all the different ways they can write about what they are learning. During this first week of the unit, usually their purpose for writing will be to capture what they are learning and what they are thinking and then writing to grow their ideas. Therefore, you will probably teach them that their notebook is a collection of many kinds of writing. You might more specifically teach them that one kind of writing-to-learn is observational writing. Students can observe a primary document, recording what they note in as much detail as possible. You might even teach them to write in paragraphs about what they have seen, using prompts like "I notice . . . ," "I see . . . ," and "This reminds me of . . ." to prime their thinking.

Then, too, as students read about their chosen subtopics, they'll sometimes find that the best way to capture what they are learning is through a sketch, and you'll want to point out that labels and captions make those sketches more informative. Conveying information through visual depiction is important from the start, because certainly children will be using visual support when they teach others about their topics in their nonfiction books. The Common Core State Standards expect third-grade informational writers to include illustrations and other text features along with the written text to help readers understand the content. The sketches and captions that your writers create now may end up being crucial components of the pages of their informational books.

Your students will also be taking notes using what we refer to as a boxes-and-bullets format, where they record a main idea and supporting facts. You may teach them to read a chunk of text and think, "What is the most important part? What facts support this important part?" Coach your writers to ensure that they aren't recopying sections from the book but, instead, are jotting quick notes about what they've learned.

You may also remind them to create annotated timelines, as social scientists do. They would take notes about events that happened in a sequence. Above the timeline, they might record facts about what happened on various dates. Below, they might annotate this timeline with their own thoughts or ideas.

Additionally, historians often use their notebooks to question and wonder. Because it is important that children continue to write with volume and stamina, you will also want to teach them to hypothesize answers to their "I wonder why?" or "How come?" musings. Teach kids to catch these thoughts by quickly jotting them in their notebooks. Then, teach them to think through possible answers by using prompts such as "Maybe . . . ," "Could it be that . . . ," "But what about . . . ," and "The best explanation is. . . ." For example, a child might look at a picture in one of her books about Italy. The picture shows a crowded marketplace with many different kinds of vendors. The caption reads, "Food is a very important part of the Italian culture." The child might write in her notebook:

> I notice in the picture that a woman is shopping in a big, open marketplace. It looks like the market-place is outside, and it is very, very crowded. I wonder why it is so crowded, is there anywhere else they can go to shop? There are many people shopping, and I notice that there are lots of men there shopping for food, as well as women, and some children are there. It looks like people are selling just one kind of thing, for example one man is selling just fruits and vegetables. There is a woman selling bread. And another man is selling cheese. It makes me think that people don't go to the grocery store like we do here to buy everything. Maybe the people selling those things made them themselves. From what I've already learned I know that cooking and making good food is really important. Maybe that's why this place is so crowded.

Nudge students to think more deeply about their topics, going back and writing about what they think about the information that they have gathered.

As the unit progresses, you'll notice that your children are beginning to have more developed thoughts, ideas, and opinions about the class topic of study. Congratulate your students on figuring out the value of writing to think about their topics. Here you might want to teach kids that historians write not only about what they observe or notice, but they also write about what they think about these observations. Therefore, you might teach kids to look back over the writing they've collected in their notebooks and write long about what they are thinking or realizing. These entries might begin with "I know some things about _____," and continue with examples: "One thing I know. . . ," "Another thing I know. . . ." This could then lead into some writing to think: "This makes me realize . . . ," "This helps me understand . . . ," "I used to think . . . but now I know. . . ." "My thinking changed because. . . ."

BEND II: PLANNING A TABLE OF CONTENTS AND WRITING CHAPTERS (AND MEANWHILE, SOMETIMES RETURNING TO RESEARCH)

Assess students' knowledge of using tables of contents to structure writing, and then teach this.

This portion of your unit will probably begin with you helping students recall what they learned earlier in the year about writing tables of contents for information books. We suggest students bring out the information books they wrote earlier on topics of personal expertise and maybe annotate those to extract all the tips they now know about how to plan a book.

While students are doing this, you can assess what they have, in fact, learned. Notice especially whether they have any sense of the advantages of a logical structure for their chapters. That is, are the chapters clumped together in any particular way? If a child wrote about soccer earlier in the year and wrote a chapter on the goalie, did that child also have a chapter on the forward? The mid-fielder? Are those chapters sectioned into a part of the book? The work of structuring one's writing in a logical order is not something that children are expected to do until fifth grade, but you will nevertheless want to note whether any of them are already doing this.

Then, too, note whether students seem aware that when they are planning their chapters, they are thinking about readers—about, as it were, the students who are hoping to learn from this information writing. Do they seem to have some sense that the decision about what comes first relates to an effort to orient and bring learners into the topic?

Finally, do students have any sense that some of their chapters will be written in a genre that matches the topic? That is, a chapter on how to get to France might be written as a how-to text.

Of course, once you have assessed your children and learned what they already know (and don't already know), you will want to jump right into teaching them how to plan a table of contents. The one caveat that we need to remind you of is this: the children will be writing about topics they are only now learning about, so part of the choice of chapters needs to reflect the information they have on hand. In part, a child's table of contents will match the subheads in the books that child is reading on the topic.

Channel students to draft chapters.

As children begin drafting chapters, you'll want to bring forward the anchor chart from the earlier unit on writing information texts and remind youngsters to do all of that work. For starters, this means that you're hoping children will recall that prior to writing an information book, it can help to teach the information to a learner, watching that learner's response so that the writer-teacher elaborates on areas that seem especially interesting, building them up to really fan the learner's interest. Then, too, the writer-teacher will want to listen carefully to learners' questions and confusions, thinking about how the information can be explained more clearly. When teaching learners, it can be useful to section off subtopics—even just using one's fingers as a graphic organizer to divide the larger topic (the hand) into subtopics (one finger at a time).

When children begin writing their chapters, you will need to help them to write in their own words, avoiding copying from their sources. You'll probably teach writers to close the sourcebook when they write, relying only on their notes and their knowledge of the topic. Of course, this will mean that writers will leave out lots of specifics, so they'll need to be encouraged to return to the source book to plug in precise names, specific quotes, and so on.

Then, too, as children write their chapters, you can be sure that they will tend to write a hodgepodge of facts. This means that you can anticipate needing to remind them of a lesson you will have taught earlier in the year. Even a chapter needs a table of contents and a plan for its structure.

You may also want to remind children of the work they did earlier on elaboration. Few things matter more in information writing, and therefore you'll want to specifically teach students to bring a variety of information into a chapter. They can look at a published text to see the sorts of information that published authors splice together when writing information texts, and they can learn to write in a similar fashion.

BEND III: USING MENTOR TEXTS TO HELP WRITERS REVISE CHAPTERS THEY'VE WRITTEN AND TO LIFT THE LEVEL OF UPCOMING CHAPTERS

Midway through the work of writing the nonfiction book (or if you intend for students to write several related books on the same topic, after writing one of these), you will want to lift the level of students' work. The most dramatic way to do this is through the use of mentor texts. The important thing to note about these texts is that they need not be about the subject on hand. These texts are mentors because of the way they are organized and written, not because they address the same topic.

Use mentor texts to spotlight structure.

When studying mentor texts, you will probably want to begin by studying the bigger aspects of these texts, such as the structure. Start off by helping your children notice the structures of these texts. If you do that, you will probably want to first study a mentor text with a classical structure.

One way to help students study the structure in a mentor text is for the class to participate in a shared reading of nonfiction. For example, you could make an overhead of two pages from a nonfiction book or place them on your Smart Board and have the whole class read the pages together. You could ask your children questions prompting them to notice how the pages are structured and the kinds of information they convey. Ask the children to talk about how they think a writer might have created this particular page, with this particular kind of writing. All the while, you can be making charts of "directions" for producing the different pages that will form their nonfiction books. A chart could have a photocopy of a page from a text with arrows labeling the different parts.

Often expository nonfiction is divided into chapters, each with its own subtopic. To produce a book like this, the writer probably learned a lot about the topic, collecting facts and ideas, and then organized those ideas into categories. Or the writer might have learned a lot about the topic, thought of categories, and then gone out in search of specific facts to fit those categories. Students will want to make sure that many of their chapters are organized according to this traditional structure.

Students may also find that some mentor texts use a compare-and-contrast structure, which is a subset of the structure described above. These chapters may have section headings such as "Similarities between Our School and Schools in Italy" and "Differences between Our School and Schools in Italy."

Yet other pages may have a narrative structure, perhaps telling a story about one particular family in Italy the child has read about, or even something more personal. Perhaps the child knows someone who has been to Italy or has visited there herself and wants to include a story about that visit.

Some books also contain chapters that are organized like opinion writing. The writer may make a claim—"Everyone should visit Italy if they have the chance"—and then the writer follows this with reasons.

The point of your teaching won't be to show students a mentor text that is structured in one way and then to assign the whole class to write a chapter using that organizational structure. Instead, the point will be that writers make choices. Writers think about what they want to say and then think about the best way to organize that content. To do this, it can help to review optional structures. You can certainly show children a few different structures during one minilesson, but your point will be that some of those structures will make sense and some will be less appropriate. You can encourage children to use the charts in the room and the mentor texts on their tables to remind them of options.

As you teach children about optional ways to structure texts, they will use this information to reread some of the chapters they have already written, deciding to revise those in ways that reflect particular structural choices. Children may even select paper that accentuates the choice of structure. They will also continue writing new chapters, and they can write the new chapters by drawing on all this new information.

Remind students that as they write new chapters and revise old chapters, they will need to return to their research and possibly do more.

Of course, to write the new chapters (and to revise the old), children will need to spend some time researching their topics, so that will also be part of what writers are doing. Whenever writers research a topic, you'll want to remind them that their notebooks are valuable resources filled with their thoughts, musings, observations, and conclusions. They could look back at what they've already written and use it not only as inspiration but also for elaboration. Or they could take detailed drawings or diagrams that they created in their notebooks and cut these out and tape them to new pages, adding lines of text on the bottom of the page. You might teach children to look back to their detailed drawings to write more on the page, or to go back to a sentence in which they used a word that might be new for their readers and write another supporting sentence defining what it means.

Use mentor texts to learn about elaboration.

You will also want to show children the ways mentor texts include a variety of types of information. Children can study a page of a published book to list the sorts of information the author has welded together, and they can compare the published book with their own writing. You will definitely want to help kids notice and then try revision techniques again—things like partner sentences (if you can write one sentence about something, you can write two or more), sequencing (going from the main idea to details that support it), vocabulary (using specific words pertaining to the class topic of study), and adding extra pages (charts, diagrams, timelines, captions, front covers, back covers, and blurbs). It's okay, and probable, that you will now reteach some of the same lessons you taught earlier, lessons from either this unit or the information writing unit.

It will serve your writers well if you spend a session on elaboration strategies, such as teaching your writers that informational writers get themselves to say more by asking a question and answering it, giving an example, and comparing or contrasting a detail to something the reader may know.

While doing this, you'll want to remind children to cite their sources. Again, the mentor text can be a source for teaching, helping children learn details about citations. While it certainly isn't imperative that third-graders learn to cite sources formally, you might want to teach them some ways to credit some of the authors and books whose information they use. You can teach them prompts such as "The book [title] says . . ." or "According to [author] . . ." to link sources with pieces of information in their drafts.

BEND IV: EDITING AND PUBLISHING TO GET READY TO TEACH OTHERS

Remind students to draw on all that they have learned about editing to get ready to publish their writing.

As the unit draws to a close, it will be important to remind your young writers that they've already learned so much about what do to fix up their writing for publication—capitalization, beginning and ending punctuation, limiting the number of *and*s in any given sentence. You can teach kids to edit their work by rereading it to make sure it all makes sense, crossing out and adding parts as necessary. Kids, all by themselves, can check their writing for frequently misspelled words and spelling patterns they have been working on.

You will also want to remind students that editing is more than spelling and punctuation—as important as those are. For example, students can reread, checking that their paragraphs each have a clear topic sentence and that the structure is clear to the reader. As part of this, you could model how you might split one paragraph into two smaller paragraphs to make each present a distinct idea.

Teach students that information writers revise with a lens for the characteristics of information writing, including headings and subheadings, diagrams, and introductions and conclusions.

Then, too, you could teach students that writers revise their headings and subheadings. Urge them to ponder, "Should a new subheading be inserted in this part of the text?"

You'll also want to alert writers to the diagrams they might have included in the text. Ask them to revise these diagrams, looking them over carefully to ensure that there are adequate captions and labels that explain each diagram clearly to the reader. "Does the diagram explain or connect to the text on that page?" children might ask themselves. "Would this diagram work better for another portion of the text? Should I shift it there?"

Teach your writers to think about the ways that the authors of their mentor texts help guide readers through the information. Your third-graders can then look back over the sections of their books, thinking about the table of contents and perhaps even a glossary they might create to help readers.

The Common Core State Standards suggest that third-grade information writers provide a concluding section. You can teach your writers to think about ways that information books typically begin and end. They might write simple beginning sections telling the reader what he or she will learn by reading the book. In their concluding section, they might write some of the reasons that the information in the book is important, or they might include some of their own opinions about the topic.

Finally, to fancy up the pieces, kids might use real photographs, just like many published information texts do. They might also add more details to their pictures and diagrams, as well as color. Kids might also boldface or underline important vocabulary.

CELEBRATE!

Set aside a special time for your students to present their information books and teach all they learned to others. They may want to visit a second-grade classroom and read parts of their books to second-grade partners, or you may decide to invite parents to come to your classroom and learn from your students' new expertise. You could set up a gallery of your students' books and invite parents to leave notes for different writers, commenting on all they learned after reading their books.

Poetry
Writing, Thinking, and Seeing More

RATIONALE/INTRODUCTION

It's hard to imagine a year-long curriculum for writing that doesn't include a unit of study on poetry. Poetry has long been the genre that human beings turn to when the occasion and the message are especially powerful. When writing for a special occasion—whether that occasion is a birthday, a funeral, a graduation, a marriage—people turn to poetry to capture thoughts that are too big for words. It's poetry that human beings learn by heart and put to music and hang on the walls of subways and classrooms.

There are more practical reasons for studying poetry as well. Although this is not one of the three types of writing that the Common Core State Standards spotlight, the adoption of the CCSS has meant that poetry is playing a far more dramatic role on high-stakes tests. Presumably because the CCSS places a premium on text complexity and asks for readers to think between the author's decisions about language and structure and the text's meaning, students are increasingly asked to engage in close, text-based, interpretive reading of poetry and to reflect on the craft moves that authors have made when writing those poems.

When approaching any unit of study, it is helpful to be clear about one's purposes. For us, a unit of study in poetry aims not just to teach students to write poetry well, but also to make youngsters into more aware and more knowledgeable readers of poetry. This unit also aims to teach children more about reading-writing connections and revision and qualities of good writing that pertain to *all* writing, not just to poetry. A unit of study in poetry writing can usher your students into a world in which reading and writing are deeply connected. From both the reader's and the writer's perspective, the unit highlights craft. For although poets write to find and communicate meaning, just like any other authors, they also, as Ralph Fletcher says, regularly "shift attention from the *what* (subject/meaning) to the *how* (language)." Fletcher's book *Pyrotechnics on the Page: Playful Craft That Sparks Writing* (2010) celebrates the ways that poetry invites youngsters to explore craft and his belief that poetry is perfectly suited to this is ours as well.

As you teach youngsters to engage in repeated revision (W.3.5) and to be conscious of craft, you'll be engaged in instruction that is fundamental to the CCSS, which expect young readers to develop their understanding and appreciation of not just what the author of a text is saying but of how texts get that meaning across. By third grade, the Reading Literature Standards state that third-graders should be able to "determine the meaning of words and phrases as they are used in a text, distinguishing literal from non-literal language" (RL.3.4) and be able to "refer to parts of poems when writing or speaking about poems using terms such as stanza and describe how each successive part builds on earlier parts" (RL.3.5). "Playing" with language in poetry, if channeled, can make children feel like insiders in this world of literary meaning making and craft.

In this unit, you'll invite children to explore the effects that are created when words are strung this way and that and repeated—sometimes even invented in response to some onomatopoeic need. Just as they learn to manipulate play dough or rearrange blocks and Legos, children can learn to take words and manipulate them to create new, interesting things: wisps of thought, a captured image, a difficult-to-describe feeling. You'll teach children to see poems, itching to be written, in the playground trees, in the recess bell and the math test, in the best friend who's moving away. You'll teach children to find the poems that are hiding in the details of their lives. You'll do all this not only because poetry is its own powerful genre but also because the habits children develop as poets—specificity, comparative thinking, understatement, hyperbole—will serve them well in any genre of writing.

There is a philosophy about learning and poetry that informs this unit. We believe that too often poetry is taught in ways that restrict and restrain. For example, in many instances, the first thing that children learn about poetry is that poems must rhyme or follow some structure or format, and sometimes children focus on these formal elements without any concern at all for a poem's meaning. We, on the other hand, think that neither rhyme nor structure should supercede meaning. Teaching form over function can backfire if children become so preoccupied with the need to alliterate and rhyme or be deliberately "figurative" in their language that they lose the heart and meaning of what it means to write a poem. For these reasons and more, this unit begins with an emphasis on meaning. We suggest you tell children, "Poets write best when they write about things they know and care about." As in previous units, you will probably want to remind your young poets that they can find significance in the big issues and ordinary details of their own lives, gathering entries and images and lists that might later be developed into publishable texts.

After a broad and welcoming invitation to come at the page from many possible directions, you will want to nudge your poets along in the writing process, showing them a few ways that they might quickly move from first tries into revision, the harder but rewarding work of pushing toward more purposeful writing. As students re-see their poems you will want to encourage them to use what they already know and have learned about revising poems. Asking students to apply what they already know invites them to synthesize, reflect, conduct, and manage their own revision process, which is work of a high DOK (Webb's Depth of Knowledge) level, where students are extending their use of higher-order thinking processes. You will want to add to their repertoire and show them that some poets sit down to write poems right away, using only a little spark of inspiration to create lines and lines of their own poetry, then going back to reread, then rewriting again and again. Other poets cling closely to published poets, reading scores of poems before writing their own, analyzing and evaluating these poems for craft moves, and may try out different versions of the same idea using different poems as mentor texts. Whatever the entry point, you will want to show your writers, through your own modeling and by looking at mentor poems and imagining the process, how to take a first-try poem, rethink it, and ask, "What am I really trying to say with this?" They can then use various techniques to tease out different possibilities, different nuances and tones that are hidden in the first draft and that take many reworkings to emerge. This deeper work in writing poems requires students to synthesize and analyze their ideas and themes in their poems, which according to Webb's DOK, engages them in higher levels of thinking.

Explained on paper, this process sounds longer than it is. In fact, you can set the goal for children to write many poems this month, encouraging them to try their hand at a variety of themes, moods, tones, and even forms. A child might decide to write about a sad or painful subject as well as try his hand at nonsense verse. Another may decide to write about some element in nature (a bird or a tree) as well as write about a person—a favorite grandparent or a not-so-favorite sibling. In addition, you might encourage children to dabble in a variety of poetic forms, both free verse and rhyming verse, for example. Once children have achieved a bit of success in their initial efforts, you might even decide to spend a small portion of the unit teaching one or two more structured forms such as haiku.

Watch for pleasant surprises from your English language learners this month. This genre is relatively flexible in terms of grammar, and poems are often shorter than prose. This can make poetry feel more accessible to ELL writers, especially if they have an internalized sense of rhythm and meter from being exposed to the richness of a poetic tradition in their primary language. Also, this genre borrows from intelligences other than linguistic. Since poetry requires a sense of rhythm, and since poems can have a lyrical quality, this genre may tap into a writer's musical intelligence too, just as the balance, precision, and symmetry in some poetic forms will appeal to a writer's mathematical sensibility. Expect your children to bring their own voices and styles to the poems that will be created in your room this month—and be ready to celebrate this voice when you see it.

A SUMMARY OF THE BENDS IN THE ROAD FOR THIS UNIT

In Bend I (Poets Live Writerly Lives, Writing about Things They See and about Which They Care), your focus will be on helping students write meaningful poems that contain content the writers care about. Students will begin writing with volume straight from the start, first using notebooks to jot down observations and then immersing themselves in mentor texts. You will want children to develop an active feel for poetry, generating and collecting lots of small blurbs that will be the fodder for their poems. Encourage them to revise on the run once they begin writing, including setting and details the way they might have done in narrative writing. Plan to spend five to six days in this bend.

In Bend II (Poets Care Not Only about Content but Also about Language and Form), your focus will shift to language and form. Students will begin rehearsing their poems out loud, reflecting on the use of line breaks—although always with an eye to meaning. They can experiment with structures such as imagery and rhyme scheme without formal teaching, learning to experience the power of poetry rather than the rote of it. Allow a week for this bend.

In Bend III (Poets Revise, Revise, Revise to Perfect Their Craft), your emphasis will be on revision. Students will engage in revision with an eye on craft moves, precise words, clear meaning, and figurative language. Encourage them to consider how their poems share messages through ideas, sounds, and visual images. If your students will benefit from a challenge, encourage them to try out standard poetic forms such as haiku or limerick. The revision work of this bend should take about a week.

In Bend IV (Poets Build Anthologies and Edit Poems before Sharing Them with the World), students will organize anthologies of poems and edit those poems for publication. They will focus especially on the sound of poetry, all affected by their deliberate revision choices concerning grammar, spelling, and punctuation. A multisensory celebration—with readings, posters, and so on—will encompass the many dimensions of poetry and your poets. Partner work will be especially helpful during this preparation for publication and celebration because children can reflect together on what they enjoy about writing poetry. It should take two to three days to prepare for publication.

GETTING READY
Gather Texts for Students

To start off the month, you'll want to create an environment in which children read, hear, and speak poetry. Perhaps you'll make fresh baskets of poems, poetry books, and collections in your classroom library. Or you might recruit the school librarian to add his or her expertise by generating opportunities for students to find, read, and reread poems they love. You will also want to gather and keep handy a core collection of poetry that creates opportunities for mentoring and inspiring students. *Honey, I Love,* by Eloise Greenfield; *This Place I Know: Poems of Comfort,* edited by Georgia Heard; *Hey World, Here I Am!,* by Jean Little; and *A Writing Kind of Day,* by Ralph Fletcher are recommended. You may want to explore the Poetry Foundation's website, www.poetryfoundation.org, which has a children's poetry section that includes children's poet laureates. An extensive list of poetry resources is also available on the Reading and Writing Project website, www.readingandwritingproject.com.

Immersion will play a larger role in this unit than in other units, from the very start and all the way through. Because you will want to teach your kids to be able to read poems well and thoughtfully and teach them how to use those poems as mentors, you will want to pick some touchstones that serve both purposes. As outlined in the CCSS, you want students to "ask and answer questions to demonstrate an understanding of a text," in this case the poems they read, and refer explicitly to the poems as the basis for their answers, "determin[ing] the central message and explain[ing] how it is conveyed through key details in the text" (RL.3.1 and RL.3.2). You will also want to select a variety of poems to share with the whole class so that you do not reinforce your kids' ideas that poetry has to look or sound a certain way. In addition to these touchstones, of course, you will need to give students access to a broader selection of poetry books or to folders containing poetry.

Use Additional Professional Texts as Needed

When designing this unit, you might need to call on some inspiration and mentors too. You can draw on professional books, including *Awakening the Heart: Exploring Poetry in Elementary and Middle School* (1998) and *The Revision Toolbox: Teaching Techniques That Work* (2002) by Georgia Heard; *A Note Slipped Under the Door: Teaching from Poems We Love*, by Nick Flynn and Shirley McPhillips (Stenhouse 2000); *Handbook of Poetic Forms*, edited by Ron Padgett (Teachers & Writers Collaborative 2000); *Wham! It's a Poetry Jam: Discovering Performance Poetry*, by Sara Holbrook (Boyds Mills Press 2002); *A Kick in the Head: An Everyday Guide to Poetic Forms*, edited by Paul B. Janeczko (Candlewick 2009); and *Getting the Knack: 20 Poetry Writing Exercises*, by Stephen Dunning and William Stafford (NCTE 1992). The poetry unit (book 7) suggested in Units of Study for Primary Writing, Grades K–2 could be adapted to older writers. You could also look to the poetry unit in the second-grade set of the series Units of Study in Opinion, Information, and Narrative Writing: A Common Core Workshop Curriculum. Visit the Reading and Writing Project website (www.readingandwritingproject.com) to find a list of other professional texts you might consider using.

Choose When and How Children Will Publish

From the start, you will want to develop and articulate a clear vision of how your third-graders will publish. You'll certainly want children to publish anthologies of poems, not just a poem or two, and you will want these collections to contain poems they have shepherded through the writing cycle. You may decide whether you imagine those anthologies having themes. If that is the case, writers may need to begin selecting poems for the anthology by midway through the unit so that they then generate more poems on their selected theme. Chances are good, though, that you'll instead suggest writers simply select their best poems for their anthologies, finding a theme or title that is broad enough to encompass all the poems.

Depending on your choice of how your poets will publish their work, you will want to spend some days at the end of the unit preparing for publication. Whether this involves creating illustrations to go with the central images of the poems they've written or rehearsing performances to deliver their poetry live or in recordings so that the meaning is clear to the audience, this will be a critical time. The CCSS states that students should "create engaging audio recordings of stories or poems that demonstrate fluid reading at an understandable pace, add[ing] visual displays when appropriate to emphasize or enhance certain facts or details" (SL.3.5). It's especially important that you teach into this a bit. In Webb's DOK rankings, these activities can be low level (if students simply make drawings for the sake of sprucing up an anthology) or high level (if you teach them to identify the most important image in the poem and create a visual of that image that goes with the tone of the poem).

Mandates, Tests, Standards

Other units often begin with an on-demand assessment that allows students to show what they know about writing in a specific genre. Poetry need not be an exception. Your children will not enter this unit empty-handed on the topic of poetry. Many will have worked on a unit of study in poetry during second grade, and the others will have been involved in shared reading of poems and songs throughout the K–2 years. You might gather your students close and say, "Writers, you are about to make an important shift in your writing lives. You are about to move from being informational writers to being—poets! As poets, you are going to see and think and write differently, because poets notice what other people miss. Poets see the world with wide-awake eyes. So when I walked into our room this morning, I looked with my poet's eyes and I realized that we have an emergency right here, right now in this room. We need poems! And not just any poems. We need the poems that only you can write. So let's take today's writing workshop to fill our room with our poems." You may want to provide paper choices for your writers—long and narrow, short and fat, with lines, without lines. You might also want to provide colored pencils so that after drafting, writers can make their poems beautiful. The children will find the day to be warm and welcoming, but meanwhile, you'll also have your pretest, and at the end of the unit, you can set aside another day for on-demand writing and contrast what your writers are able to do then, as poets, with their efforts today.

As you study your children's earliest efforts to write poetry, notice what they seem to think makes for a good poem, and let them influence the way you teach your unit. Writing poetry requires a balance between thinking about content and thinking about language, between thinking about meaning and thinking about form. If children lean too much toward one extreme or the other, they will need your teaching to support balance.

Then, too, writing poetry requires both a playfulness and a seriousness. Poems should be fun and, in a way, easy to write, but students also need to feel as if writing poetry requires a writer to rise to the occasion. You'll want to assess whether children's expectations are too high or too low and help to make them just right.

BEND I: POETS LIVE WRITERLY LIVES, WRITING ABOUT THINGS THEY SEE AND ABOUT WHICH THEY CARE

Immerse students in poetry, and use that immersion to spark early drafts of poems and entry blurbs about possible poems they could write.

Your month-long unit on poetry may begin with what will probably be a two- or three-day period in which students generate lots of early drafts of poems and entries, or blurbs about possible poems they could soon write—all collected in their writer's notebooks. In this way, you will teach students that writers use their notebooks to begin collecting drafts of poems and ideas for poems.

One of the best ways to help children generate ideas for poems they can write is to invite them to read poems others have written with a pen in hand, ready to write their own poems or jottings in response. You might invite young children to join you in selecting poems that could turn the classroom and the school into a poets corner. Perhaps they'll want to put poems in places they frequent: "Pencil Sharpener," by Zoë Ryder White, can be posted by the pencil sharpener; "The Drinking Fountain," by Ken Nesbitt, can be mounted near the drinking fountain in the hallway; other appropriately themed poems can be displayed in the cafeteria, near your classroom library, next to the clock or the nurse's office or the bathrooms—anywhere your students might spend a little time. The important thing, however, will be for children to not just find poems to hang, but for them to then read those poems with notebook in hand, writing poems in response to the posted poem, or writing entries that could be any collection of images or ideas.

You will also want to read poems aloud in ways that create the mood and set the tone for your writers. You can say to your children, "Listen as I read this, and then afterward, in the silence, let's all pick up our pens and write, write, write. The room will be absolutely silent. Just the scratch of pens. You might write a poem in response to what you hear. You might write a personal narrative, or just thoughts or images. Whatever you write will be something you can revisit later and see if, perhaps, in that material, you find something remarkable."

Then you'll read, and you and your children will write. During this generating phase, you'll probably not alert children to particular craft moves that poets make. That will come later. Instead, in these initial two or three days, you'll immerse children in the genre so that they develop an active feel for it and channel them to write snippets of thoughts and bits of poetry into their notebooks—lots of them.

After children find and read poems for a few days and collect their snippets of poems and thoughts, you'll definitely want to teach them that rereading what they've collected is a wise thing to do. "Flipping through the pages of your previous writing might lead you to poems that are hiding in the words, waiting to be written," you might say, urging your young poets to take their pencils to previous notebook entries, circling or copying out a line or a paragraph that they might turn into a poem. Of course, children should reread all of their previous writing, not just what they have done at the start of this unit, looking for seeds of poems. Demonstrate how they might identify a section in one of their narratives or information books or feature articles that has a clear idea or that expresses a strong emotion or insight. Show how this might be lifted out, set onto the top of a new page, and then written about, again and again.

You may be asking, "What exactly are children writing at this stage?" You are right that we are being vague, but that is partly on purpose. You'll want to let children know that there are a variety of ways to write poetry. Some writers start by writing prose and then mine that prose for poetry, and some write rough drafts of poetry from the start. The important thing will be the exploratory feel to the early writing that children are doing—and also the volume of it. A little five-line poem will not be the work of one writing workshop! Instead, imagine that every child is writing at least a page full of snippets during any one day's workshop, with that page containing at least three different poems or snatches of writing.

Teach students that as poets they should pay close attention to the world around them and the feelings inside.

You may want to teach writers that sometimes it can help to walk around with one's notebook in hand, looking for poems. To bring home that idea, you might bring your class on an observation walk (this could be a nature walk, a community walk, a school building walk) with notebook and pen in hand, helping them to observe and write in response. It will probably help for you to teach them first to write long about what they see, what they notice, and what this makes them think. Above all, you will try to teach—and model—a thoughtfulness and a wakefulness that is essential to getting a poem going. "Look at this sky!" you might exclaim during a nature walk, throwing your head back to marvel at the streaks of cloud and the vivid blue above you. Say the visual words that occur to you out loud: "Blue—so blue—cloud shaped like a kangaroo." Nothing you say need be very poetic or profound as long as you uninhibitedly model a sense of being alert to the visual details around you.

Varying the theme, you might read aloud a poem or two that express a strong emotion, telling your readers, "Poets pay attention to how things make them feel. They then write these feelings down." You might follow this by showing them a few visuals (slides or photographs) and asking them to look at these through the lens of how the picture makes them feel. Suggest that they try jotting more than just the feeling (happy, sad, worried) by also jotting what the visual reminds them of. Encourage association of one image with another remembered image or anecdote. These associations ("This reminds me of . . . ," "This is just like . . .") will help your young poets come up with other images and pave the way for thinking more figuratively.

Just as some poems originate in ideas and images, some begin, quite literally, with words. A catchy phrase or a lyrical line can play in a poet's head and eventually spur a bigger, binding idea. Many teachers start a poetry unit by bringing in song lyrics and inviting children to bring in the (appropriate) lyrics to music they are obsessed with. This is a way both to notice how songs are really poems (including line breaks, repetition, figurative language, rhyme schemes) and to use lines in songs to inspire new writing based on the same theme or image.

Early on, you might also encourage children to talk with a partner and then write reflectively about notebook entries they collected earlier: *I'm writing about this because . . .* ; *This is important because . . .* ; *I used to think . . . but I learned . . . so now I think . . .* ; *I want my reader to feel or think . . .* ; *One thing that may be missing here is. . . .* This work helps children uncover the deeper meaning in their entries and prepares them to select entries that are calling out to become poems. It's especially important to teach into this reflection work; in Webb's Depth of Knowledge rankings students will be working at level 3 as they analyze, explain, and evaluate their notebook entries to create ideas for poems. Other good prep work is to have students start thinking early about how these budding poems might have similarities and how they could potentially become poems for an anthology that they might develop.

After a few days of generating or collecting, your writers will have lots of small blurbs and/or first tries, all waiting to become poems. These entries are initial fodder for powerful poems. The next job will be for writers to turn the blurbs and tries into more polished poems, and this will be the second part of Bend I.

Teach writers that poets revise from the start, turning paragraphs and jots into early drafts of poems.

A mid-workshop teaching point or a share during these first couple of days could introduce the idea of on-the-run revision. Although the third bend in this unit focuses on revision, don't wait until then to recruit your students to revise. Let them know, instead, that poets don't wait until "revision" time to rethink and recraft something they're working on. It's always revision time in poetry. Right away, you can look at the lines you just wrote about a visit to the ER in the night.

> I had to go to the hospital
>
> in the middle of the night
>
> for them to check my breathing.
>
> I was so scared,
>
> and so was everyone else.
>
> But none of us said anything.
>
> I wish I had spoken to the boy next to me.

You can quickly try to add an image from the setting or a detail about an object or piece of clothing that will make this poem more piercing. In doing this revision work, students are meeting the CCSS Language Standards, specifically, "demonstrat[ing] understanding of word relationships and nuances in word meanings" (W.3.5), which helps them to choose words that create specific moods or evoke strong reactions in their own poems. You can especially look for a surprising detail or one that adds a new emotion to the poem. You might remind children of how, in personal narrative, in fiction, in informational writing—in every kind of writing—they worked on bringing in important details. Poetry is no different. So you might close your eyes and picture the waiting room at the hospital and end the poem this way.

> Most kids were there with family
>
> hugging them and cheering them up.

One boy, a teenager, sat alone,

no family, no one at all. His leg

shook as he tapped his foot.

I wish I had spoken to him.

According to Webb's Depth of Knowledge, as students are making these quick revisions they are doing high-level thinking, because they are engaged in transference and are using what was taught the month before or even the year before.

Partner work will be important during revision. Partners can help each other by giving feedback and even recommending next steps. A poet who has written about the loss of her dog in a story poem, for example, might read the poem to a partner, and the partner might say, "Is there an image of your dog that comes back to you over and over? You could try finding that image and repeating it." In other words, partners can coach each other to try out the teaching you've already done. As partners are preparing for feedback they are, of course, reading texts, revising poems, and strengthening their speaking and listening skills. The CCSS call for students to be able to "ask questions to check for understanding of information presented" (SL.3.1c) and "ask and answer questions about information from a speaker, offering appropriate elaboration and detail" (SL.3.3).

Teach students that revision will lead to more intensive rehearsal and drafting.

As the first bend progresses and children go from collecting to revising their earliest bits, you'll want to also remind them that everything they do to make poems better should help them to collect seeds of poetry that are even more promising. The unit will be cyclical, with children continuing to live like poets throughout, so after a bit of time reminding youngsters that writers revise and getting them to do that, you'll also want to remind writers to go back and collect more entries, living their lives with the wide-open eyes of poets. If your students participated in the second-grade poetry unit from Units of Study in Information, Opinion, and Narrative Writing: A Common Core Workshop Curriculum, they carried Tiny Topics notepads with them for just this purpose. One teacher described it this way: "Poets see both the big and the small, they notice great big issues and ideas that other people haven't realized yet. They also see the smallest little details that other people just walk by. When you are out walking around, you might stop and see a crack in the sidewalk that no one else is noticing or think about how everyone is walking around so fast and no one is stopping to talk. All of these things you might quickly jot down."

BEND II: POETS CARE NOT ONLY ABOUT CONTENT BUT ALSO ABOUT LANGUAGE AND FORM

Introduce students to line breaks and structure, teaching them how the decisions they make accentuate rhythm and meaning.

This bend will help youngsters to draft and revise poems with an attention to form as well as meaning. By the end of Bend I, children will have written something like eight poems. In this bend, they'll revise the poems that they like and write a whole lot more.

Don't let the focus on form lead you to think right away that you'll be teaching writers a particular form—haiku, for example. Nor will you want to begin with rhyme. Instead, you will probably want to begin by teaching children to write with line breaks that accentuate their meaning and that help the poem "sound good." Teach children to aim first for meaning and for finding a way to describe what matters with words that will make the reader see the world in a brand-new way. You might teach writers that when poets turn prose into poetry, they try to discover rhythm in the sentences they've jotted. For example, you may put one of the blurbs you wrote up on chart paper or the document camera and read it aloud.

> I remember when I was at the park with my little sister. Normally we would fight a lot. One of us always wanted to get on the slide first. But this one time, my sister saw a worm. "Look," she said, "it's like a jungle snake." I went over. "Ahh! A snake! Oh, no!" I said and pretended I was afraid. That is when she grabbed my hand and said, "I'll save you." I looked at her and smiled. I was really happy she was my sister.

"This is not a poem," you'll tell kids. "But I can find the rhythm in these words—break the prose into lines—and convert it into a poem. When I take a sentence and break it into lines, poets call those places *line breaks*. I can mark the spots with a little slash. I know from the poems I looked at that sometimes lines breaks happen at end punctuation, sometimes they happen at important words, and sometimes they just happen when it would sound good to pause. I'm going to add a few and then ask you and your partner to help me." You might turn back to the chart and begin adding slashes, all the while thinking out loud about your decisions.

> I remember when / I was at the park / with my little sister. / Normally / we would fight / a lot./

You could then ask students to help you add other line breaks to the poem. Next, show your class how you can quickly rewrite a draft of your poem, going to a new line at each slash mark.

> I remember when
>
> I was at the park
>
> with my little sister.

While you write, you might think about your mentor texts and decide to experiment with the same blurb again, but in a different way. Usually, when students feel that each try is just experimenting, just playing around, there is a lot more freedom—even willingness—in their choices and in their attempts. Utilize minilessons, conferences, small-group work, and partnerships to provide students with support in developing and strengthening their poems (CCSS W.3.5). You will decide which kinds of work to demonstrate for your whole class, which are good for small groups or individual conferences, and what order feels most appropriate. Beginning with more structural changes will help students very quickly see their potential as poets.

Experimenting with making lines and stanzas will quickly create the visual look of a poem. Noticing how poets often do not write out full and complete sentences, instead eliminating extra words and getting right to the important stuff, will also quickly help your children see themselves as poets. For example:

Going from:	To:
I remember when	I remember
I was at the park	the park
with my little sister.	my little sister

Teach students that poets use imagery and rhyme schemes to help their readers better understand what they are trying to say.

In addition to structure, students might experiment (at this point rather freely and loosely) with imagery or rhyme schemes, which they will develop further during revision. "Poets sometimes create powerful pictures," you might say, perhaps introducing the academic term *imagery* and explaining that poets, just like other kinds of writers, often create images to help readers better understand what they are trying to say. All the while, continue to help your students look back to the mentor poems for examples and inspiration.

You will want to teach children the power of metaphors and similes by studying a few examples of them. Your point now will be that writers use literary language to make comparisons in ways that help them say things that aren't easily said in regular language. Your goal is to invite children to feel comfortable trying out and using literary language. You might, for example, teach children that a powerful way to create "mind pictures" is to place an ordinary thing next to something it's never been compared with before: "Today the sky looks soft and worn, like my old baby blanket." Save a further discussion of rules and definitions until later in the unit, after they have fallen more in love with this craft strategy.

This work of noticing poets' craft moves guides students to think more deeply about using specific words to convey meaning, distinguishing between literal and nonliteral language, rather than trying to fit their poems into specific structures (CCSS RL.3.4). We have all read student poems that, for example, make rhyme far more important than substance: "My mom is nice / I like to eat rice." Or poems that have so much onomatopoeia that you can barely make sense of what is going on: "Smash, boom / Gurgle, splat."

The danger is that students will start plugging craft techniques into their poems just because they can, not because it really matters to the meaning they are trying to convey.

BEND III: POETS REVISE, REVISE, REVISE TO PERFECT THEIR CRAFT

Remind children that they can bring forward revision strategies learned in other units and use those strategies to revise their poems.

By now, children will have written and revised something like a score of poems. This bend provides you with a time to teach writers how to revise a smaller number of poems deeply, using deliberate craft moves.

Not surprisingly, you'll start this work by reminding children of revision moves they have used in earlier units. If children are accustomed to revising the lead, the ending, and the heart of texts, why wouldn't they do that work with poetry? If they are accustomed to noticing what an author has done in a published text and trying that same craft move in their own text, why wouldn't they do that in their poetry?

As children do that, they will also be thinking about whether the qualities of good writing that they have already studied pertain to poetry. For example, earlier in the year, when writing narratives, children learned that instead of summarizing, it is usually more powerful to story-tell. That's applicable to poetry as well.

There are also lots of revision strategies that are especially suited to poetry, though again, most of those strategies could be used in any genre. "Poets whittle away excess words, deliberately choose the tone and mood they want, and find words that match their meaning, or insert figurative language." You will want to draft a poem or two of your own in front of the class and use them as models on which to demonstrate each revision strategy. In each case, you'll want children to see clearly what you did, how they might do the same, and also that this move made the poem visibly better.

For example, one revision lesson could focus on how alternative titles can enhance the meaning of a poem by adding more to the ideas, being more literal than the rest of the poem or even setting up readers to expect one thing and then be surprised when the poem goes in a totally new direction. As readers of poems, your students also no doubt have already learned how beginnings and endings play a huge role in the poem's meaning; they can now put great care into the construction of their own. You might teach them that the last moments of a poem are like a gift to the reader, how they usually leave a final special image or contain the poet's big idea or comment about everything that came before. This can be surprising or beautiful or moving. Just like in narrative and essay writing, your young poets will want to try out various ways their endings could go. As your students are using multiple revision strategies to convey ideas and themes, they are thinking and writing with a deep awareness of purpose and audience. This is central to level 4 in Webb's Depth of Knowledge.

Encourage partnerships to help each other organize and strengthen their writing through planning, revision, and editing (CCSS W.3.4 and 3.5). As students meet with their partners to read and revise their poems, you will want to urge them to play with punctuation. You will want students to challenge one another on the true meaning of their poems. If they want the mood of the poem to be sad, they might decide that it is best to have fewer exclamation points ("Exclamation points make everything sound upbeat and exciting, so they won't fit here.") and more periods and perhaps a dash to show long pauses. Students might plan to use commas to break apart a list of things or to add more detail-supplying words: "The bright, yellow leaf died / as it drifted, softly, quietly to the ground."

You will also want to teach children how the poet quite deliberately crafts the tone of a poem and how word choice plays a large part in creating that tone. Read a few poems out loud and ask children to identify the tone of each before examining more closely how the poet crafted this tone: the words, the punctuation, the line breaks will all have played their part. This is a good time, also, to chart "degrees" of verbs for students to refer to as they make word choices. For example, create a chart that lists different words they can use instead of *walk*, such as *trot*, *tiptoe*, and *stroll*. In this way you are not only teaching word choice but also helping children learn new vocabulary. Often, third-graders spend time adding adjectives that don't necessarily create a vivid image. Teach students to abandon overused adjectives such as *beautiful* and *pretty* and focus on using precise description. "The beautiful bird" could be changed to "the gray and white striped bird." You are really teaching children to write with precision—a skill they need in any genre.

Channel students to use ideas, sounds, and images to convey meaning.

As your young poets revise, it might help them to think about the ways poets share their messages with readers: through ideas, through sounds, and through visual images. Teachers in previous years have sometimes categorized their revision strategies in these ways, both in their instruction and on charts posted in the room. Children can try to create sounds in their poems to further express their thoughts and feelings and discover how their lines could have rhymes between them or even within them. You might show them published poets who are really skilled at rhyming, such as Jack Prelutsky, and teach your students that to rhyme is a choice, not a requirement of poetry. Which words to rhyme is a more important decision. Prelutsky often chooses words for comic effect. In his poem "My Parents Think I'm Sleeping" he rhymes the word *gone* with *flashlight on*: "I was quiet as my shadow / till the moment they were gone, / then I dove beneath the covers / and I snapped my flashlight on." Other sounds are important too. You might go back to one of your own mentor texts that you read aloud and look again with your class at how long vowel sounds can have a very different effect than short, choppy, hard consonant sounds. They might also revise for the sounds of their poems by looking again at the choices they are making with repetition and punctuation, both of which can change the way lines and stanzas sound. Your young poets will hardly be able to contain the urge to read their poems aloud, and partners can help a great deal here—either listening or, better yet, reading the poem back to the poet to see whether the words he or she wrote make a reader hear the sounds the way the poet hoped.

Poets also convey their ideas visually, and as they revise, children can decide how long or short their lines are on the page, whether there are stanzas and how many, which words are capitalized, and what punctuation to use. They will learn how poets use the white space around the words to pause, take a breath, and make something stand out from all the other words.

Now that students have learned to focus on meaning, introduce a few standard forms of poetry.

Revision is a perfect time to look at a few standard forms of poetry, though it is probably not necessary (or wise) to attempt to teach every (or even any) form unless you feel that both you and your students will benefit and be interested. Once students have lived with their entries for some time and have worked on many different permutations and mined them for meaning, inviting them to experiment with how, say, a limerick, haiku, or pantoum might enhance what they are trying to say can feel really powerful and now purposeful. Choosing to work on form near the end of the unit, not the beginning, means that students are making choices about how and when to use a certain form, versus simply filling in blanks to get the right number of syllables. For instance, the entry about going to the park with your younger sister might be really beautiful as a haiku now that you understand what you are really trying to say.

Always we would fight.

But, when a pretend snake came,

my sister saved me.

BEND IV: POETS BUILD ANTHOLOGIES AND EDIT POEMS BEFORE SHARING THEM WITH THE WORLD

Guide students as they choose which poems they want to publish and how the poetry will be celebrated.

As you approach the celebration, you may invite your poets to make choices about how they will share their poems with others. In some classrooms, students decorate the poems and post them in public places throughout the school and the neighborhood. In others, students read and perform poems, both ones they've written and those published by their mentors—not only in the classroom but also in the larger community. Still other classes create poetry anthologies.

If you decide to encourage your children to publish anthologies, you'll want to teach them to look at all their different poems and consider how some of them might fit together. Some poets do this within themes; we might notice that many of our poems are about family or about feeling proud or about an important place. Writing partners are very helpful during this phase of the writing process. Questions to ask a writer to help him or her choose poems to publish are:

- Which of your poems do you like the best? Why?
- What are some different ways you could group your poems together?
- What kind of poetry writing did you enjoy the most?
- Which images do you love?

As children assemble their poems, they might also decide to include the mentor poems they used or other published poems that fit the theme.

Teach students that when poets edit their writing, they have to make decisions about what conventions they will follow, always keeping their readers in mind.

Of course, as children prepare for publication, they will also need to edit their writing and to learn about how poets edit. Editing poetry, at first, can feel a bit like an oxymoron. How do you teach students to look for rules of standard English when poetry breaks so many of those rules? Although poetry can break rules, no one poem breaks all the rules; otherwise, readers could make no sense of it. So you may want to tell your writers that poets edit with their readers in mind. They make purposeful choices about what kinds of grammar, spelling, and punctuation rules they are going to follow and, if they choose not to follow some, what alternate rules they *will* follow. For instance, a poet might decide that at the end of every idea she will not use a period but will instead go to a new line. When she edits, she'll check that she always does this. Or the poet might choose to capitalize following standard rules and check for this. In other words, you'll teach children to edit their poems for consistency in the grammar rules they've chosen to observe.

Editing in poetry is also about sound. Children will probably read their poems aloud several times, checking each time whether they included all the marks, line breaks, and kinds of words that make their poems read just as they want them to sound.

Regardless of how students choose to publish, remember that the secret of poetry is heart. Poets write from the heart. Poets teach all of us to look at the world differently. They help us celebrate small beauties. They inspire us to be outraged over injustices great and small. Therefore, as this unit draws to a close, focus on the work that poets do in the world, the way poets love the world through words. Focus on the way poems sustain us during hard times, the way poets express outrage and grief and joy, how poems can connect our hearts and minds to one another.

The Literary Essay

*Equipping Ourselves with the Tools to Write Expository
Texts that Advance an Idea about Literature*

RATIONALE/INTRODUCTION

This unit builds the groundwork for the fourth-grade unit *The Literary Essay: Writing about Fiction*. That fourth-grade book teaches students to write literary essays that develop strong interpretive theses about literature, are well organized, use textual evidence efficiently to support a claim, and focus on characters and their traits. In that fourth-grade unit, students read and reread a familiar short story, then a familiar novel, and eventually they work across texts. In this way, they progress from simpler, more straightforward literary essays to those built around more complex theses to compare-and-contrast essays. Writing to defend claims about literature requires close reading, attention to literary craft, and the ability to cite and defend relevant textual evidence. For this reason, many of you may decide to expose children to literary essay writing in third grade. This unit is meant as a precursor to the fourth-grade book *The Literary Essay: Writing about Fiction*. The unit aims to make reading a more intense, thoughtful experience for children by equipping them with tools they need to write simple essays that advance an idea about a piece of literature. This unit relies on children's prior experience with opinion writing, suggesting that instead of writing about opinions such as "It is important to recycle," they can now write about claims such as "Winn-Dixie teaches people to care for each other."

MANDATES, TESTS, STANDARDS

The Common Core State Standards (CCSS) emphasize the importance of teaching children to read closely to determine what a text says not only explicitly but also implicitly. That is, in third grade, students are expected to refer explicitly to the text, demonstrating an understanding of the text (RL.3.1), and by fourth grade students are expected to draw inferences, citing details and examples to support the claim (RL.4.1). Similarly, the standards ask that children learn to analyze and interpret texts, analyzing "how and why individuals, events, or ideas develop and interact over the course of a text" (Anchor Standard R.3).

The CCSS is also clear that students must have the ability to write arguments about topics *and texts* (the expectation of the first Anchor Standard for College and Career Readiness). This unit offers students the chance to begin developing their skills at essay writing; in particular, it will support them in transferring and applying all they have learned in *Changing the World: Persuasive Speeches, Petitions, and Editorials* to now write simple essays about texts. The unit also gives you a chance to shore up the elements of argument writing about which your students are unsure. You will want to have all of your data from across the year at hand to ensure that you are helping students move along a trajectory of work and make progress in large, visible ways.

A SUMMARY OF THE BENDS IN THE ROAD FOR THIS UNIT

In Bend I (Close Reading to Generate Ideas about Literature), you'll teach children that just as essayists pay close attention to their lives, literary essayists pay close attention to texts. Children will select a text from several they are familiar with and generate lots of entries about it. You will teach them to mine the text for ideas, pulling out a favorite passage or line and explaining why that passage stayed with them after they were finished reading or why it is so powerful or how it relates to the rest of the text as a whole. They will then elaborate on these ideas, expanding their thinking so that you can then channel them to choose one seed idea and write a thesis statement that they can grow into an essay. You will probably want to spend only several days in this bend.

In Bend II (Support and Craft the Arguments), children will gather evidence to support their claims, elaborating on and crafting their arguments. You will scaffold children's work as they draft, revise, and edit their essays, working hard at retelling important moments from the text, angling their essays to support their claim, crafting their introductions and conclusions, categorizing their evidence, and incorporating literary terms. This bend will be quick, lasting only several days, to leave time for students to cycle through the writing process again in the final bend.

In Bend III (Draft and Revise Essays with Increased Independence), children will draft a second (or third) literary essay, this time doing so with increased independence. You will want to raise the level of your students' work by having them transfer and apply everything they learned in the first two bends of the unit to this new essay. You might decide to spend a shorter or longer amount of time on this bend, depending on how your students did cycling through the first two bends, though we recommend moving quickly, having students flash-draft and then revise on the run, before editing and publishing their final piece to great fanfare and celebration.

GETTING READY
Gather Texts for Students

For children to write about reading this way, you will need to decide which piece(s) of literature your children will study in the unit. If your students are in a reading workshop and talking about the deeper meanings of texts in book clubs or partnerships, you might use literary essays as a way to harvest their interpretations of those books and to cross-pollinate your reading and writing workshops. On the other hand, book club work is not essential to this unit. Your students might write literary essays about any short story, novel, or picture book that you and the children have discussed.

You will want to choose the easiest possible texts for children's foray into literary essays. It is reasonable to ask whether writing about chapter books or picture books is an easier challenge. In some ways it is easiest for children to write about a short text; in other ways this is more difficult. Certainly when youngsters write about a short text, it is easier for them to know that text really well, rereading it several times and mining it in conversations with others. They can also locate evidence easily without spending lots of time finding excerpts. On the other hand, any theory a child might espouse will have thinner substantiating support when the text is short. For example, if a child claims that Gabriel, in the three-page story "Spaghetti," by Cynthia Rylant, is lonely, there will be very few bits of evidence the child can draw on to make his case! It is far easier to supply evidence supporting the claim that Opal, in *Because of Winn-Dixie,* by Kate Di-Camillo, is lonely.

You will need to decide whether children will write literary essays about short texts they have read during writing workshop or about longer texts they have read and discussed during reading workshop. For our purposes here, we'll assume they are reading short texts (but we have no bias toward this). If you make that choice, we recommend that you provide children with a small folder containing a few possible texts, letting writers select the one that "speaks" to them. Be sure you include a text or two that are easy enough for your struggling readers. When writers have choices and can write about topics they care about, the writing is better. In this instance, the writers' first choice is the text; their second choice is what to say about it.

The texts you offer as options should be ones you and your class have studied throughout the year. There is nothing to be gained by introducing unfamiliar ones. Provide stories that are rich, complex, and well-crafted enough that they reward close study. *The Stories Julian Tells,* by Ann Cameron, offers a collection of good options. Eve Bunting's picture books are also very rich. The possibilities are endless. You will also probably select one mentor text for whole-class work, threading this one short story through many minilessons, using your (and the class's) responses to it to show children how people go about reading, thinking, and writing about a story. You'll chart what you do with that story, using words that can apply to any writer and any text, and those charts will remind children of the work they can do with their own stories. Again, one way to support children who struggle is to do some work with the text that you hope they will use as the centerpiece of their inquiries.

Anticipate the Trajectory of Your Students' Work throughout the Unit

You will need to decide from the outset how much time you are going to spend in each part of the unit. The unit is meant to be a quick one, with a week on the first two bends. You can decide how long the final bend should be. It could be longer. In any case, we recommend finishing the unit by having your students write at least one and probably more fast drafts of literary essays.

However you proceed, plan to celebrate the children's achievements at the end of the unit. You might have students lay their first and second literary essays side by side and visit one another's writing, complimenting as they go. Or you might set up a rotating display in the classroom that highlights the books as well as the essays, with the literary essays tucked inside the books about which they were written. You might also give the students' opinions a larger, broader audience by posting the essays on Goodreads.com or another literature blog.

BEND I: GENERATE IDEAS ABOUT LITERATURE

Channel students to write lots of entries about a selected text.

On each of the first few days of the unit, you might decide to demonstrate a way of reading and writing about a story and then invite children to use that way of reading as they work with whichever text they choose from their packets. (Ask children to make that choice right away, so all the writing they do over the next few days sets them up for the essay they will soon write.) You might teach children that just as essayists pay attention to their lives, expecting to generate ideas from this wide-awake attentiveness, literary essayists pay attention to texts. It is particularly effective to teach them that a reader can capture an image or a line or a passage that stays with him after he finishes reading a story and then try to explain why that one bit of the text is the part that lingers in his mind. How does that one part fit with the whole story?

Because text citation is so important to the CCSS, you would be wise to teach students that writers can pull out one line or a couple of lines of text and copy them onto a page of a notebook and then write to help them figure out why they found those words or that part so powerful. Again, it will be important for writers to explore how the statement fits into the story as a whole.

You might also teach writers that it can pay off to record a turning point in the book and explore how this moment fits into the whole book or to write about how they might live differently if they took the story really seriously. Of course, you will not want to suggest a strategy, show it, and then expect every writer to use that strategy to explore a text. Instead, you will want to teach a few strategies for growing ideas about a text and then invite writers to draw from that repertoire of possible strategies, using one, then another, as they see fit. It can help to teach writers that there are tricks to anything, and one of the tricks that a literary essayist calls upon is that she knows in advance that there are some parts of a story that tend to provide a rich ground for analysis. These potentially rich parts of a text include moments of character change, the lessons characters are learning, and the issues (personal or social) characters are facing. As always, you will only want to devote a day or two to teaching students strategies for generating ideas about their reading, and then you'll want to help them write well about those ideas.

By now, you will want to lift the level of your students' writing about reading. As part of this, you will probably encourage them to go back to entries they have written within the last week and elaborate on these. This means that you might channel children to select bits of *their* writing—whole entries or portions of an entry—and try to elaborate on those ideas, just as they earlier selected bits from the books they are discussing. For children to say more about a text, encourage them not only to think more, but also to see more. They should be growing their ideas by studying the text, noticing evidence for their ideas, and thinking about that evidence. That is, if writers select the text fairly early on, the generating and collecting they do henceforth will be work that sets them up for their eventual essay. Your next mission is to help them grow and eventually choose between some ideas about the selected text. Writers can look closely at the text they've selected and write, "I see . . . ," followed by something that they notice in the text. Encourage them to write long about this, extending their observations by using prompts to jump-start their thinking: "This makes me think . . . ," "I wonder . . . ," "The surprising thing about this is . . . ," "The important thing about this is. . . ," "The thought this gives me is. . . ," "I wonder whether. . . ."

Children are used to extending their thinking by providing examples. Support that work, and help them to mine those examples for the specific ways they actually relate to the initial idea. Simply referencing an example is an important part. Including a line that reads, "This shows . . ." and then showing how the example illustrates the point is much better work.

Be aware that children are apt to try to extend their thinking only by providing examples; therefore, you will want to encourage them to linger with their ideas, too. Teach them to record an idea using new words, writing, "That is . . ." or "In other words . . ." and then rephrasing the idea. Teach them to entertain possibilities by completing the prompts "Could it be that . . ." or "Perhaps . . ." or "Some may say that. . . ." Words and phrases such as "Furthermore . . . ," "This connects with . . . ," "On the other hand . . . ," "But you might ask . . . ," "This is true because . . . ," or "I am realizing that . . ." can also keep children elaborating on their ideas. If you hope that children will write literary essays in which they articulate the lessons they believe a character learns or name the theme or idea a story teaches, it is important that you provide children with strategies for generating these sorts of ideas.

You might use fantastic writing about ideas generated by some of your students as powerful mentors to help all your writers visualize what it is you are pushing them to do. These entries may also inspire you to create minilessons that spotlight your students' work. You might consider making a mid-workshop teaching point in which you ask the class to analyze what makes the work of one of their classmates shine. This will help them articulate the moves they too should be making in their writing.

As your students continue to elaborate, you will want to remind them of the ways they are already familiar with for thinking about characters and the work they do as readers. You might ask them to revisit any writing they have been doing all along about their reading, asking themselves, "What ideas have I grown already about this text?"

Have students decide on one idea to develop into an essay.

Next you will want to teach children to reread their notebook entries to find seed ideas. You might ask them to look for a seed idea that is central to the story and is provocative. You can also help children generate possible claims or thesis statements or ideas about the text. Whatever structure a child chooses, you will need to help him or her revise the seed idea so that it is a clear thesis—a claim or an opinion, not a fact, phrase, or question.

Before teaching into this work, you need to know that the Common Core State Standards expect students to write opinions or claims and to supply reasons or examples to support the opinions or claims but do not expect third-graders to coordinate all those layers of development. That is, according to the CCSS, it is okay for a third-grader to claim that Opal, in *Because of Winn-Dixie*, is lonely and then to elaborate on this by telling about three *times* when she is lonely or, alternatively, about three *ways* she is lonely, but the CCSS do *not* expect third-graders to write with a cascading organizational structure, which might lead to the child claiming in her thesis statement, "Opal is lonely for two reasons. She is lonely because her father has what he thinks are more important things to worry about and therefore largely ignores her, and she is lonely because she is only just starting to build a life in the wake of her mother's death," and then to develop each of those reasons with several examples. This type of organizational structure, where the writer plans the entire essay up front, laying out the reasons that support the thesis or claim in the thesis statement and then elaborating on each supporting reason in the body paragraphs is what is expected of fourth-graders according to the CCSS. The organizational structure that is expected for third-graders when writing about reading is no different than what they did when writing essays in the *Changing the World* unit. It is entirely okay for a child to make a claim, come up with one reason, write about that reason, and then only at that point think, "What other reason can I come up with?," adding a transitional phrase and then continuing with the next reason.

Still, there are ways it is just as easy for writers to make a claim that, from the start, meets requirements for fourth- and fifth-grade CCSS. Some of your writers might make a claim about a character or a text, perhaps giving reasons for that claim straightaway or perhaps doing so as they proceed along, writing the essay. "So and so is a good friend." "So and so changes the family [the town, the classroom, the school] from this way to that way." "This is about so and so, who learns/turns out to be/changes to be/becomes such-and-such by the end." For example, "*Because of Winn-Dixie* is the story of a lonely girl, Opal, who learns that she isn't alone after all." Or "'Spaghetti' is the story of a lonely boy, Gabriel, who learns to open himself to love."

When children go to elaborate, one of the easiest ways for them to do so is to divide their essays up so they write about how their ideas hold true across the text. The first body paragraph can claim, "In the beginning . . . ," and then the next can start, "Later in the text . . . ," and of course, the final body paragraph can start, "By the end of the text. . . ."

Alternatively, writers may want to write "journey of thought" essays: "At first I thought . . . but now I realize. . . ." Students may write, "When I first read [story title], I thought it was about [the external, plot-driven story], but now, rereading it, I realize it is about [the internal story]." Or "Some people think [story title] is about [the external plot], but I think it is really about [the deeper meaning]."

Other students may want to write a thesis statement like this: "My feelings about story/character/theme are complicated. On the one hand, I think . . . On the other hand, I think. . . ." With this structure, students can explore how their feelings or ideas about a story, character, or theme are conflicted. The reader feels more than one thing at the same time. "My feelings about Jeremy in 'Those Shoes' are complicated. On the one hand I think he is generous and selfless, and on the other hand I think he cares too much about what others think."

Implicit in many of these thesis statements is the plan for the essay, but remember, this is not essential for third-graders. Still, if the statement is "My feelings about such-and-such are complicated," then "On the one hand, I think . . ." and "On the other hand, I think . . ." become the topic sentences for separate paragraphs. If the thesis is "At first I thought . . . then I realized," those elements, too, set up the organizational structure of the essay.

BEND II: SUPPORT AND CRAFT THE ARGUMENTS

Teach students to find evidence.

Once children have planned their literary essays, they will need to collect the information and insights needed to build the case. You might decide to encourage each child to make a file or a booklet (on which they write on one side only) for each big subtopic the child plans to discuss in the essay. For example, if the child's claim is "Cynthia Rylant's story 'Spaghetti' is the story of a lonely boy who learns to love," the child might title one file "Gabriel is a lonely boy" and another "Gabriel learns to love." Each of these files will become a paragraph (or more) in the final essay. On the other hand, students can work their evidence into their draft immediately, one paragraph on one page and another paragraph on another page.

You might teach children to gather evidence for each subordinate point by retelling a part of the story that supports that idea, then "unpacking" that part by writing about how it illustrates the idea. If you teach them to do this, you will need to help them angle their retelling so it fits the idea. You will also need to teach writers how to quote from a text and then unpack the quote by talking about how it addresses the relevant big idea. Before this unit is over, you may want to teach children that writers of literary essays use the vocabulary of their trade, incorporating literary terms such as *narrator*, *point of view*, *scenes*, and the like.

Have students put it all together and revise.

There are several alternatives for how you might teach children to take what they have collected and turn it into a cohesive essay draft. First, you'll want to teach children to lay all their evidence before them, determining which stories, quotes, and bits of expository writing best support their ideas. Then, using only what they decide to include, writers can literally construct an essay by taping the pieces together. You'll want to teach them to use transitional phrases at the beginning of paragraphs and between examples. This may be something you teach them as they draft or save for a revision minilesson.

Alternatively, you might have children fast-draft their essays. They'll still lay their evidence before them, choosing the best pieces for their essay, but instead of eliminating and taping, they'll reference this evidence as they draft their essays from beginning to end on lined paper.

When teaching children to write introductory or concluding paragraphs, you'll want to remind them that essay writers state their opinions and forecast or sum up their reasons. You might teach them to write an introductory paragraph that includes a tiny summary of the story and then presents the thesis statement. The closing paragraph will probably link the story's message to the writer's own life. It's a good place for a Hallmark moment! ("This story teaches me that I, too . . .") An alternative is to link this story to another story or even to a social issue in the world. Also, as students revise their essays, they will want to read their drafts carefully—most likely with a writing partner—looking for places where there are gaps (in thinking or transitions) and filling those gaps as they revise. You'll also want to study your students' writing in relation to the opinion learning progression and note places where their essays are still in need of work. These "needs" become perfect revision strategies.

Finally, of course, you will want to teach your writers a lesson or two about editing their essays. First, you will build on the editing work children have done throughout the year, encouraging students to make smarter and smarter choices about paragraphing, ending punctuation, and the like. This is also a great opportunity to teach verb tense, which often switches during an essay. That is, when children are discussing their thinking, they sometimes use present tense ("Gabriel is lonely."), and when they are retelling, they sometimes switch to past tense ("Gabriel saw the cat."). This can be confusing for your struggling writers, and you will want to be prepared to help them make good choices—and understand the choices they are making.

For a celebration of this first round of writing, you might have students share their writing with a small group and write quick compliments to each other. You might also consider making copies of their essays and tucking them into the book baskets in the library. As students go to a bin to pick a book, they can read a bit of their classmates' thinking about the story.

BEND III: DRAFT AND REVISE ESSAYS WITH INCREASED INDEPENDENCE

Cycle children through the writing process again, with increased independence.

You will now want to spend a few days cycling your students through a fast version of the literary essay process. If your students did well the first time around, you'll make this bend as independent as possible. Allow children to choose the books they will write about, and remind them of strategies for collecting ideas and evidence by hanging the charts you created earlier in the unit. Encourage students to develop a thesis quickly, moving immediately to the collecting of evidence. In this third bend, you'll want to give them increased choice. Some children will create files again. Others may simply make little booklets (a few sheets of paper stapled together, their thesis on the first sheet, their first reason across the top of the second sheet, their second reason across the top of the next sheet, and so on).

Strive to raise the level of the work children are doing. You'll certainly want to teach children to use the opinion checklist to assess themselves. Teach them to note what they've done well and what they still need to work on and then set goals they can work toward. Remind them to use the various strategies you taught in Bend II, this time with increased autonomy and independence. We recommend keeping this bend rather short; the goal is to usher children *quickly* through the literary essay process. However, if your students struggled significantly in Bends I and II, you might decide to slow down and reteach some of what you introduced a week or two ago. Regardless of the approach, students will end Bend III with a second draft. Plan to both celebrate and reflect on these drafts. If children leave this unit with clear goals in mind for essay writing, they will be well positioned to make a smooth transition into fourth-grade essay writing.

Revision

RATIONALE/INTRODUCTION

The Common Core State Standards (CCSS) mention revising and editing as important elements of the writing process. And any time that we ask students to reconsider their work, to pause and read back through and try to lift the level of it, we are in fact helping them work toward a higher level of thinking.

Many students view revision as a quick fix in the writing process—a place only to change a word here or add a sentence there. While revision does exist on the word or sentence level, you will want your students, as they become more proficient, to see revision as reworking or revisiting entire parts and, ultimately, the whole of a piece.

This unit will provide your children with a chance to take the time to step back and reflect on what they have done and then dive back into previous work with new vigor, making shapely and significant changes. You will encourage them to look over their entire collection of written work and think about how they can make work they wrote earlier even stronger. This sort of self-reflection, so crucial to Charlotte Danielson's work, increases students' ownership over their own learning. Children will have grown as writers and as people since they wrote some of the pieces from early in the year, and it won't be hard for them to imagine new possibilities for those pieces.

If this unit is coming toward the end of the school year, as we imagine, you can tell children that the purpose of this project is for them to end the year with a collection of finished work that represents their writing for the entire year. This then means that children can also have motivation for revision. Now is their chance to show the world all that they have learned to do.

A unit on revision is also a unit on independence. Your writers won't all be doing the exact same kind of revision work. Although the unit will channel students to work for a time revising narrative writing and for a time revising expository writing, within those broad constraints children will still be working in different genres and at different paces. This means that they will need to use their entire repertoire of strategies. They will need to think not about what the class is doing, but instead about what each one of them needs to do individually. They will need to look over their writing and ask, "What is it that I will work on now?" Then, they will need to execute that plan. They will, of course, have the support of your minilessons, charts, and the other writers in the room. However, now more than ever, they will steer their own ships, deciding when to move on to the next piece and when to linger.

Creating a space for this kind of independent work will foster writers who take up their pens at any time of day, look at their writing and the world around them, and then begin a writing journey. This work will support children in creating writing plans for themselves and seeing those plans through. You will want to foster this motivation to write and to create writing projects for themselves. As children look ahead into the summer, you will want to set them up to keep their own writing lives going. By teaching students to work with independence on projects they select for themselves, you are supporting them living writerly lives throughout the summer. If we build a community of writers who are excited to take this work on, then we are working toward preventing summer writing loss.

A word about this unit before you proceed. We've included this same unit as an optional unit within the fourth-grade book as well as this book, and we are aware that the way we have written this is ambitious for third-graders. You may well approach the unit planning to lean on the broad plans for it but planning to alter the qualities of writing that are taught so that you use the unit as a time to reinforce anything your students seem to you to be needing. For example, you may see from the checklists that across the board, they need more work on endings, and therefore you might make that an important part of this unit. Always, whenever you teach, tailor units that we outline so they support the specific children in your class.

A SUMMARY OF THE BENDS IN THE ROAD FOR THIS UNIT

In Bend I (Rallying Students to Revise and Building Up a Basic Revision Toolkit), children are reminded that revision is a crucial stage of the writing process, that it separates "drafters" from real writers. Students will collect their best pieces of writing from work they have done across the entire year—probably choosing previously published texts (and some entries) that feel worthy of revision—and they will place these in a special revision folder. They will then be reminded of some of the basic, most essential of all revision strategies, such as trimming their writing down to the clearest and strongest words, adding details or examples where elaboration is necessary, and writing with a sense of audience. They'll begin revising many of their selected pieces with these strategies in hand. Plan to spend about a week helping your class to revise up a storm.

In Bend II (Deep Revising within a Community of Writers), students will choose one piece of writing from the folder of "good enough to revise work," and they will revise this one piece of writing in far deeper, more meaningful ways than is usual. They'll do this, in part, by asking, "What is the big thing I am trying to say? What message do I hope readers will take away from this?" Students will develop this core meaning, discarding chunks of text that take away from it and creating new text that adds to it. In this bend, support from a writing community (partnerships and clubs) will scaffold children's individual revision efforts. The second bend will be apt to last about three days.

In Bend III (Revising Narrative Writing), students will specifically revise one piece of narrative writing they produced earlier in the year, with an emphasis on the qualities of good narrative writing that they have learned. Specifically, they will focus on story arc, pacing, sequence, character development, setting, leads, and endings and will study mentor narrative texts to find inspiration for revising toward a specific effect. Above all, they will examine their work through a critical, revisionist lens. The bulk of this unit will be spent in this bend, perhaps devoting a week and a half to this.

In Bend IV (Revising Expository Writing), students will specifically revise one piece of expository writing that they produced earlier in the year, with a special emphasis on structural clarity, paragraphing, sequencing, and following the thread of a unifying thesis statement (in the case of essays) or a heading/subheading (in the case of other information writing). They will also learn to revise with attention to the use of transitions or linking phrases to connect the thoughts within their writing. This bend is shorter than the previous ones and should only take about two to three days to work through.

In Bend V (Editing and Celebrating), students will consolidate all of their revised pieces and edit these for final publication. The focus will be on revising spelling, mechanics, and punctuation (proofreading their own—and perhaps a neighbor's—work), reflecting on what kind of writers they are and what kind of habits they need to build to become more effective. Students will also reflect on their growth and their process from initial drafting to final revision and editing, to take charge of their own future learning and move toward independence. At a final celebration, students will have the opportunity to share their before and after pieces with their classmates and even next year's teachers. This celebration doubles as an affirmation of students' work and an informal time to create continuity between grades. This is yet another short bend in the revision road and should only take about two days.

GETTING READY
Gather Texts for Students

It will help you to retrieve mentor texts that you have used across the year and perhaps add to that collection with a few new mentor texts. You will need to have on hand both narrative and expository texts.

Use Additional Professional Texts as Needed

There are many useful professional texts on revision. You may want to consult Ralph Fletcher and JoAnn Portalupi's books on revision, *Craft Lessons* and *Nonfiction Craft Lessons*, as well as Georgia Heard's *The*

Revision Toolbox (it's not just for poetry). For your own reference, you may also be interested in Roy Peter Clark's *Writing Tools: 50 Essential Strategies for Every Writer* and Don Murray's *The Craft of Revision* or his classic, *A Writer Teaches Writing.*

Choose When and How Children Will Publish

Since there are many bends to this unit, you may want to break it up by having a mini-celebration at the end of Bend III, after students have spent significant time working with narratives from earlier in the year. You don't need to make a big affair of this. Perhaps you will set up a revision museum, where students lay out their revised pieces, in all their flaps and spider leg glory, for all to see. You could also have children set their mentor texts side by side with their revised drafts, illustrating the crafting techniques that they have incorporated into their own writing.

You can use your end of the unit celebration as a time for reflection. Students should be given the opportunity to think about how much they have grown as third-grade writers. The original writing and the revised writing, side by side, is tangible evidence of this. You may also want to invite fourth-grade teachers to the celebration as a sneak peak at the writers who will be gracing their classrooms the following year.

Before students begin any revision work on their selected pieces, you will want to make photocopies and set them aside to be used at the celebrations.

BEND I: RALLYING STUDENTS TO REVISE AND BUILDING UP A BASIC REVISION TOOLKIT

> Some of the best writing comes when you rehash. It's in the retelling of stories that the improvement comes. The reflection comes in the polish. What a person will see, what a person will feel, comes in the polish. When you finish polishing your writing, it forms the image you're trying to create.
>
> —Donald Perry, freelance writer and author

Generate excitement for revision work by teaching students that real writers revise. Immerse them in the revision process.

You'll want to start this month by recruiting youngsters into becoming purposeful, independent revisers of their own writing. The tone you set at the very start of the month is important. Remember, it might not be altogether thrilling for children to dig out old pieces of writing and look at them afresh. You don't even want to give them the chance to protest, "But we're done with these!" To offset this possibility, you'll tell them right from the start that this month they'll be doing work that separates the "real writers" from the "first-drafters," that the core and secret of powerful writing lies in revising, that this is what serious, professional writers do *all the time*. It might be helpful to display what real writers (especially the kind who children recognize and love) have to say about revision, for example, the following quotation from Roald Dahl:

Charlie and the Chocolate Factory took me a terribly long time to write. The first time I did it, I got everything wrong. But the story wasn't good enough. I rewrote it, and rewrote it, and the little tentacles kept shooting out from my head, searching for new ideas, and at last one of them came back with Mr. Willy Wonka and his marvelous chocolate factory . . . and then came Charlie . . . and his parents and grandparents . . . and the Golden Tickets . . . and the nasty children, Violet Beauregarde and Veruca Salt and all the rest of them.

Or the following quote by Judy Blume:

I'm a rewriter. That's the part I like best . . . once I have a pile of paper to work with it's like having the pieces of a puzzle. I just have to put the pieces together to make a picture.

Youngsters will have grown as writers from earlier in the year. "The older you will always revise the younger you," you might teach. "That is as true in writing as it is true in life. You are smarter, more mature writers now than when you wrote many of these pieces." In this unit, you will expect youngsters to look critically at their own earlier work and self-assess how they might bring up the level of a piece of writing.

It will help to clarify the gist of revision by modeling the process in a brief, straightforward way. Immerse students in examples of revision by showing them how you revise stories from previous units of study, how past students revised (by showing a sample of a former student's work) and by revising class stories together. If you wrote a class story or two in the first few units on chart paper or a transparency, you can have students join you in revising the class story using a variety of strategies. You might even place before and after revision pieces side by side to demonstrate a clear improvement in quality.

Make sure that this initial modeling is simple and that it offers dramatically visible results. Youngsters need to see that revising is an instantly effective process, that it can make a general word more specific, a rambling sentence more concise, a scattered chain of thoughts more streamlined, an ordinary sentence extraordinary. The purpose, at this early stage in the unit, is not necessarily to have children imitate your revision moves as much as it is to prove the meaningfulness of this month's important work and to recruit their enthusiasm for wanting to do it.

You'll also use the start of this unit to set up a revision center in your room, complete with the tools and materials that will aid in the work that children will be doing in this bend and throughout the unit.

Channel students to reflect on their writing year, making decisions about which pieces they want to move to their revision folders to work with further. Guide them to self-assess their writing and come up with their plans for next steps.

Once you have your youngsters on board, you'll want them to reflect on this past year of writing, reading and rereading their own work, including previous notebook entries, drafts, and published pieces. You'll also want children to ask themselves, "Which piece do I want to revise?" These can often be the best, most developed pieces, ones that children have invested thought and heart into creating. Note that the least successful writing pieces may not be worth deep revision, even if it seems there is much to revise in them. You can teach children to select pieces that have hidden potential, where meaning is not yet evident but can be clearly developed. "What might this piece be about? Can I bring this meaning out?" is one way to look at an entry. Another is to ask, "Is the meaning clear? Will the reader understand what I'm trying to show? Is there a way to make this more gripping, more interesting?" Sometimes, rereading a piece will inspire a new thought, a new idea, or a new story, and youngsters might even recognize this inspiration right away. "Sometimes a piece of writing literally pops with potential," you'll want to tell them. "You might reread and realize there are some other, new things you want to add. Maybe there are entire paragraphs you want to replace." Children may even begin their revision work by actually writing long in their notebooks about why they want to revise this piece and what they want to change about it.

At this point in the year, students will have cycled through several units in many genres and will have plenty of strategies to turn to. You'll want to haul out the archived genre charts, process charts, and rubrics from units past and display these in your room. The narrative and information learning progressions, for instance, can be very helpful in enabling children to self-assess and to articulate and plan the next step. In all of your teaching, but especially in this unit of study, it is critical to help students cumulatively apply all they've ever learned about the qualities of good writing.

Instruct students to place the pieces they select in a special revision folder. While they will be picking multiple pieces to revise, since this is a multigenre unit, you'll urge youngsters to pick at least one piece each of narrative and expository writing to work with in later bends. While it is possible to teach generic revision strategies for all genres together (as we do in the first two bends), we have structured this unit so that Bends III and IV separate narrative revision from expository revision. Your students should easily recognize the differences in the ways narratives and expository texts are built and will benefit from learning revision moves that are specific to each genre. Before students begin any revision work on their selected pieces, you will want to make photocopies and set them aside. When you come to the final unit celebration, you will want students to be able to set these copies side by side with their revised pieces to get a full sense of the work they have accomplished.

Teach general revision strategies that work across genres: decluttering, revising sentence structure, and considering audience.

In this first bend, children may pick up and revise lots of pieces of writing, regardless of genre. You'll help youngsters to build up a basic revision toolkit comprising the most basic, nonnegotiable revision moves that all writers build into their process. The first of these is the removal of deadwood from their writing. Call it tightening, decluttering, paring, simplifying, or hacking and slaying, the process is the same and applies across all genres, for writers of all ages. It requires cutting and discarding the inessential word, sentence, or paragraph. Most, if not all, first drafts contain words that do not add to meaning, that simply take up valuable space. You'll teach children various ways to declutter their paragraphs and sentences. Teach children that one may, in fact, cross out an entire paragraph—even two—after asking, "Are they really necessary?"

Another way to teach decluttering is to demonstrate how a writer can cut out repeated ideas and repeated words and phrases, or demonstrate replacing a group of words with a single, precise word. So, "They walked all the way up to the top of the mountain" could easily be "They *climbed* the mountain." Similarly, "She walked silently, trying not to make a sound with her feet" might easily become "She *tiptoed*." You'll want to explain that in writing, less can be more. One more way to explain decluttering is to teach youngsters to revise their writing at the word level, taking out redundant words. Demonstrate that many adjectives and adverbs are dispensable where they repeat the effect of the word they are meant to describe, for example, *wet rain, shining sun, tall skyscraper*, where the adjectives do no work because rain has never been dry, the sun has never stopped shining, and skyscrapers can't be short. Similarly, *smiled happily* doesn't say much more than *smiled*.

Partnerships can be used to support this work. You might set partners up to read each other's writing, lightly parenthesize a "dispensable" word or idea, and hand it back for the writer to consider whether the word can actually be dropped from the writing. This is the process that William Zinsser describes in *On Writing Well* as something he did with his graduate students' writing while teaching at Yale. Third-graders can do this work just as well, once you demonstrate the effectiveness of this practice and empower them to take their own words seriously.

While revision certainly involves taking the unnecessary "stuff" out of a piece of writing, it can also mean inserting some important parts into our writing. You'll want to show children that revising can mean adding an example or a detail that will make a point or an image more specific for the reader.

Similarly, you can also teach children to revise sentence structures to avoid monotony. Third-graders often write an entire paragraph that follows a monotonous series of subject-verb sentences, for example:

I went to the mall with my family. We ate ice-cream. My sister spilled some ice cream down the front of her shirt. That was her best shirt so she started bawling.

You'll want children to recognize monotony when they read it. Read out the start of each sentence to demonstrate the pattern that needs to be broken: I-went, we-ate, my sister-spilled, that-was, she-started. Explain that this is the kind of pattern that works like a lullaby, putting readers to sleep. You could teach children to revise in ways that break such monotonous patterns by beginning a few sentences with a verb (action):

Spilling ice cream down the front of her best shirt upset my sister.

Or you could teach them to liven up their prose by inserting dialogue:

"It's ruined! My favorite shirt! Waa," my sister bawled at the top of her lungs. People turned to stare.

Audience is another reason to revise: we revise when we have in mind a particular person or group of people that we know will be reading our work, keeping in mind the effect we want the piece to have on that particular person or group. To instill a very real sense of audience, you might go so far as telling kids that all their revised work will go immediately to their new teacher as an introduction to their writing, or you could plan a celebration where they will present their work to the incoming third-grade class. You may give children the opportunity to choose an audience for their pieces, either in addition to or instead of the whole-class publishing, thereby letting them decide who they want to read their pieces and why.

Prepare your writing center with revision materials, as well as scaffolds for how to use them.

Early on in the unit, you'll also want to create a writing center that supports revision by laying out various materials and tools. These might include strips of paper to add sentences and sections into the middle of students' writing, flaps of paper to tape over discarded parts, single sheets of paper to staple onto the end or the middle parts, Post-it notes, tape, staplers, correction fluid, colored pens, and scissors. You may want to create a chart for the writing center that lists the tools, how the tools are used, and what revision strategies they support. For example, you might list "strips of paper" and then describe a use of paper strips—to add details. You can describe strategies for how to insert dialogue, internal thinking, or physical description when adding details so that kids know to use them for specific reasons. This will help shift the focus from the strips and toward revision strategies. Invite students to create their own revision tools and spotlight the ones that seem to be working well, sharing them as an example for other students to follow.

BEND II: DEEP REVISING WITHIN A COMMUNITY OF WRITERS

Teach students that writers evaluate the purpose behind their pieces before revising. They think about what they want to say to their readers and then use this to guide their revision decisions.

In this bend, youngsters will select a piece or two of writing (in any genre) to revise more deeply. This could be a piece they already worked on in Bend I, but if it is not, you will, of course, expect for them to carry forth all they learned from the first bend about removing deadwood, audience awareness, and so on. In this bend, however, you will teach revision as a means to achieve a far deeper investment in writing. Deep revision involves evaluating the very purpose of a piece of writing, and this can result in substantive changes to the original content. Children (like adult writers) are sometimes so proud of the way that a word or sentence looks on paper, or so impressed by the sheer volume of what they have written, that it can be hard to let go. In this bend, you'll teach youngsters that writers are ruthless with the work that matters most. Real writers don't just trim a word here and add a comma there. They stand back and check: "Is it working? Does it all go together? Is it the absolute best it can be?" And then they make big decisions.

In every stage of the writing cycle, purpose is key. This holds true tenfold for revision. In this bend, writers will evaluate the purpose behind a piece of writing. Writers often reread something they've written and ask, "What am I really trying to say?" or "What is the one big thing I want the reader to take away from this?" Often, the writer will see a section that seems to be standing separately or a part that doesn't quite go with the rest. This is a time for decisions. Should the writer stick to the original idea that he started with? Or should he allow a tangent to develop into its own—possibly bigger, better, stronger—piece?

The answers to such questions will be far clearer when you model the way you tackle these in your own writing. You'll pick up a simple text that you might have created with the whole class earlier in the year or create a new one especially for the demonstration of this teaching, for example:

Cats are amazing creatures. The cat family consists of leopards, lions, cheetahs, even jaguars. Did you know that ballet dancers are inspired by the way that cats always land on their feet? It's true. If you throw a cat into the air (though you shouldn't) it will always land delicately on its feet. Cats are so graceful. My aunt has the video for a musical called "Cats." My favorite of all is Rum Tum Tugger. He always does the opposite of what is expected of him.

You'll want to model your thinking as you revise this piece. "What is the one big thing I'm trying to say?" you'll ask. "Is this piece about cats—the animals? Or is it about *Cats*—the musical? Those are two separate things. One is an essay, and the other is a story about 'a time when.' I'm going to confuse the reader like this." You could show children many ways to proceed from there. "Do I want to make this an All-About cats text? I will have to make a decision and then cross out the part that is irrelevant. I could cross out the All-About and just write longer about the musical and about Rum Tum Tugger, for example." You could then proceed to cross out the discarded part to demonstrate the finality of such a decision.

But you also want to show youngsters that a writer works with several options. "Writers, if I want to keep both parts, I have to show how Rum Tum Tugger connects with my 'all about cats.' Maybe I can add":

People who keep cats as pets might agree that all cats are like Rum Tum Tugger. They seldom do what their human owners want them to.

You'll want to explain, "Writers, this will still take some work to become smooth. But at least it is no longer two different things. It is an All-About cats text where Rum Tum Tugger becomes an example, a piece of supporting evidence for the fact that cats are stubborn creatures."

You can teach youngsters to think purposefully, envisaging the effect they want to achieve with a piece of writing (perhaps using some other text as a mentor) before jumping into specific craft moves that will help them make the required changes. You might suggest that writers read their work aloud, and they may try first revising by varying their reading tone of voice, then changing the writing to match the tone they like the best. They might even try having their partner read the piece aloud as they listen. These moves will help writers embark on purposeful decisions about what they want to say, the tone they want to use to say it, and the effect they want to have on the reader.

Immerse children in a writing community. Teach them how to use partners and revision clubs as a resource for their revision work.

During this bend, you'll also want to set up ways for youngsters to accept and provide revision support to peers. This unit is a great opportunity to show students that strong revision lies not only in their own solitary processes, but also in the thoughts and feedback of a writing community. You will want to offer students opportunities to share, talk, and revise with others. There are many different ways this might go. You might choose to teach a revision strategy in a minilesson and then send kids off to talk and work with partners on how they could try the day's strategy before independent writing. Kids might discuss places where they could try the day's strategy, work together to make writing plans for the period, or help each other get started. In this case, partners would confer prior to writing as a way of planning for revision. Alternatively, you may teach a revision strategy, send students off to write independently, and then schedule time for partnerships to meet at the workshop's end. You might teach students to share how revision strategies are helping the piece, to share before and after versions, or to share their further revision suggestions.

Remind children that they don't need to take all of their partner's suggestions and that a suggestion is a recommendation, a possible way to go, not a command. Ultimately, partners have the opportunity to read and reread their stories together, thinking more deeply about their pieces. The Common Core State Standards expect that by third grade students do not solely rely on teachers for feedback, but also use "support from peers" to revise their writing and move their work through the writing process.

You might want to explore various opportunities for grouping children in this bend and throughout the unit. Oftentimes you'll take this upon yourself, organizing students who have common needs. For instance, you might form a small group of students who are revising essays, another group of students who are working on a collection of pieces, and another group of students who are using mentor texts to revise. Other times, you'll want to support students in making their own grouping choices. You might encourage them to find partners who are working on similar kinds of pieces or revising using specific strategies. You might have one group of writers who are helping each other resequence their stories, another group that is studying leads, and yet another group that is focused on taking their pieces and rewriting them into a different genre.

Regardless of grouping, give children time at the end of a work session to talk in their clubs about what they tried, what worked, and with what they're still having trouble. Another way you can support the focus of the club is by requiring that they "workshop" one writer's piece each day. So one writer will share his work on Monday, another writer on Tuesday, and so on. This way there is a sense that the whole club will focus on one writer's piece, as well as an understanding that every writer is expected to open up her work to the club.

Clubs may want to choose a mentor text in their genre to serve as a guidepost for their revisions and talks about their writing. Children may choose from touchstone texts that you've read as a class, from the narrative learning progression if they're in narrative writing, or from other sources that you may have available to them in folders organized by genre. During the first days of club work, kids may spend time at the end of the writing workshop reading the mentor text as writers, to construct their own language for what they want to try in their writing based on their mentor author's work.

BEND III: REVISING NARRATIVE WRITING

Have students focus on revising narratives using the narrative checklist and general narrative structure.

By now children should have a clear sense of the revision process. In this bend, you'll teach them to revise *narrative* writing specifically. Ask them to select a narrative piece from the start of the year to revise. Presumably, they will have just recently written fairy tales, so you can help them to contrast their start of the year personal narrative with their best fairy tale, asking them to think about what they learned to do as fairy tale writers that they might be able to use to revise their personal narrative story, making it much better.

You'll also want to highlight the narrative checklist that documents what third-graders should already know (it is a version of the CCSS) and be able to do as narrative writers. They can assess their narrative pieces against that checklist and make goals for what they still need to do to make them as strong as possible. You might show students a child's text that matches the third-grade narrative standards and one that matches the fourth-grade standards (and the checklists) and challenge them to revise their selected pieces so that they are at least meeting third-grade (and possibly fourth-grade) standards.

You might begin by reminding students of the general narrative structure: that time moves across a story arc featuring characters, setting, conflict, climax, resolution, and lesson learned. You'll remind children that a narrator/storyteller's job is to carry the reader through a scene (and into the next, if the story contains two scenes) across the arc of the story, showing rather than telling, zooming in at specific parts, and moving quicker over others.

To make your teaching effective, you could at some point introduce an underdeveloped narrative as a demonstration text. That is, you may share a Small Moment story with your students and then, over the course of the bend, revise and develop this story to demonstrate various teaching points. For example, if your teaching deals with developing the heart of a story, then you could visibly ponder over your own Small Moment story and think aloud each step in a way that reveals to youngsters exactly what kind of decisions might go into developing this heart. "Sometimes, writers realize that the way they wrote something doesn't match what they really intended to say. In narrative writing, this often happens if a scene doesn't quite come alive in full detail for the reader or if the heart of the story doesn't seem important enough."

Another possible revision for narrative writing is to think like a movie director and decide where to pan out for a wider view and where to really zoom in on a tiny detail. There may be places where a sweeping view of the whole of a scene might be particularly effective, such as looking across the entire lunch room and noticing all the tables crammed with kids laughing and eating, and other places where the close-up of a trembling hand might tell the story best.

Teach students to revise based on common elements that are seen in narrative stories—character, setting, and sequence of events.

Since children are revising stories, you will want to help them refine and polish the most important aspects of their stories. One story element you might help them with is character development. "Writers can revise a character to make that person seem so alive that he or she jumps out of the page," you might teach. "One way to really bring a character to life is to bring that person to the center of the stage and let her start talking. Just as we can tell so much about a person from the way he speaks, we can tell about a character from her choice of words and her mannerisms." Read out loud direct dialogue from classic mentor texts to demonstrate how this helps the reader envisage a character. For example, you could pick up a Beverly Cleary book and read aloud practically any character's words to instill children with a realization of authentic character voices: Imagine Dad, when he says, "Ramona, my grandmother used to have a saying. 'First time is funny, second time is silly, third time is a spanking.'" Ask third-graders, "What is Dad's mood here?" Or read aloud a few quotes from the mouth of Ramona Quimby herself, that most distinctive of characters.

"Please pass the tommy-toes."

"If I can put butter on my mashed potatoes, why can't I put jelly? I put butter and jelly on toast."

"I am *not* a pest."

Point out that Ramona's voice is recognizably different than Beezus's voice and that the direct words each character uses help a reader imagine each one better than any adjective can! You might have a little fun with your active engagements, inviting one partner to write in the distinctive voice of one or two specific classmates and having the other partner guess who. Suggest that writers come to know a character's quirks and habits in the same way that we know our own friends and that writers allow these characters to bring their own distinctive voices to the paper.

Similarly, you might teach students to revise their stories with a particular emphasis on setting. You'll teach that descriptions of setting help situate the story and bring a scene to life for the reader. Explain that events are defined by the time and space in which they occur, that a story moves the reader from scene to scene.

Again, mentor texts are invaluable in demonstrating how the setting provides more than just a passive backdrop for a story, how in fact, it sets the very mood of the story. Prompt your writers to ask themselves, "Where does this character live? Where does this story take place?" and to consider setting as more than merely a geographical spot by posing a question like "What is the *culture* of this place?" You might explain this by referring to your own city (an area with which children are familiar), asking children to ponder how one neighborhood or shopping area can be culturally different from another. Urge them to think, for example, how a small-town greengrocer or a discount store are different from a gourmet supermarket. You might challenge students to "show" the setting by providing specific details rather than by "telling" the reader about this setting using lazy adjectives. For example, telling the reader that "it was a tiny, cramped room" is not nearly as effective as showing them.

"There was no place to put my feet because every inch of space had been taken up by stacks of books, odd furniture items overflowing with dust-encrusted odds and ends, pencils, yarn, chewed up toys, a broken pair of spectacles. . . ."

You may teach children to reconsider the sequence of their stories, thinking about where to build suspense, where to start, and where to end, and then use revision strategies for resequencing, including cutting and stapling. Adding details is an important part of revision. Children can reread their pieces and think about which parts of a piece are the most important sections, and they can elaborate upon those sections. If kids are having a hard time determining the most important part of their story, they might ask themselves, "Where in my story do I show the biggest feelings or the most important ideas?" For example, a student rereading his story about cooking *arroz con pollo* with Grandma on Saturday could realize that the most important part happened when he and his grandmother smelled something burning. He would then decide to develop this part of the story, adding dialogue and small actions that show his feelings. You can teach strategies for adding more details to the text using strips of paper in the middle of sections. It is important to teach children the reasons for altering a draft, as well as to teach the physical work of revision.

Use mentor authors as models for revision work.

You may also want to teach children to review their leads and endings. Show kids that they can try writing a few different versions of any part of their story and then think about which version works best. To write new leads or new endings, children can study previous mentor texts, or new mentor texts you introduce, naming what the author did that the child might emulate. For example, children might reread the ending of *Fireflies* and recognize that Julie Brinckloe ended her story with a strong feeling. Kids could then try to write similarly in their own pieces. They might notice that an author began her story by describing the setting and try to write similarly.

Mentor authors will play a large role in this unit as students pore over texts that will help them improve their pieces. You'll want to show students how they can study a published text that resembles what they are trying to produce. You may decide to pull out a few great fiction picture books and help your young writers see how this author crafted the details to bring out the internal journey of the main character. All of this work will support the Common Core State Standards for reading, which require that third-graders discuss craft within a specific scene and notice how subsequent scenes build upon each other.

Most importantly, you will want to teach your writers that they must find their own mentor authors, combing through the baskets of your classroom library to find a text that they would like to emulate. While it will help them to watch you point out authorial choices and craft moves, it will create even greater independence if you teach them how to notice great writing on their own. You might suggest that your students read like writers, noticing particular parts that work well in these published texts and then asking themselves, "How did the author do that? How might that go in my piece? Where could I use that language in my writing?" You can model for students how once you've noticed great writing in another text, you can return to your own draft and revise with that particular lens. Although this will happen in writing workshop, this work supports the Common Core State Standards that call for students to notice authors' word choices and discuss the intended meaning and effect.

Coach students to think about their writing from their reader's point of view. Writing partnerships and clubs can help with this work.

As youngsters revisit the narratives they've written, shift them into the perspective of the reader so that they pay attention to parts where the reader will need to envision and predict or anticipate what happens next. Partnerships might help with this, where youngsters read over a friend's writing and point out a part that leaves an unanswered question or a part that feels like it might need further elaboration.

Again, as in the previous bend, you can set youngsters up to work in clubs. This provides immediate feedback, support, suggestions, and accountability. Clubs can discuss strategies, such as adding a setting by creating a movie in their minds, remembering where the characters were and what was around them, and then adding description. By discussing the specific revisions they could make, children are more apt to follow through with what they said. You might choose to showcase strong examples of partner and club work by asking children to gather around a club and listen to its conversation, naming the positive qualities they might replicate in their own partner work.

Celebrate the work thus far with a revision museum.

There are many bends in the road of this unit, and your students have spent significant time revising their narratives. This would be a good time to stage a mini-celebration. This should not be anything grand; save that for your end of the unit celebration. One possible way for students to publish their writing could be to have a revision museum. Students can set out their revised narratives side by side with the photocopies you made of the original narratives. If there was a particular mentor author that they emulated, a specific page in a mentor text that highlights a crafting technique that they replicated in their own writing, the mentor book could also lie side by side with their writing. Give the class an opportunity to take a museum walk, chatting with each other about what they are noticing and about how much more powerful their revised writing has become.

BEND IV: REVISING EXPOSITORY WRITING

Teach students that when revising teaching texts, writers evaluate their texts for clarity and expository structure.

The chance to revisit some of the essays and informational writing that they've produced throughout the year can actually be an extremely valuable learning experience. No longer are youngsters collecting and sifting through miscellaneous information or their own thoughts about a topic. No longer are they researching or trying to teach. A revisionist stance can actually free children to stand back and look at the expository texts that they've already created to evaluate their overall structure and effectiveness.

You'll want to urge your writers to step inside the shoes of their readers and try to experience their own writing from a distance. Remind them that the first question that a reader asks is "What is this text trying to teach me?" Writers will want to evaluate their own texts for clarity. One way to be very clear for the reader is to follow a predictable expository structure. Ask youngsters to identify the expository structure that their writing follows: Is it boxes and bullets? Is it cause and effect? Will the structure be easy for the reader to identify?

While revising structure, expository writers will also want to ask:

- Is there a clear theme that threads throughout the essay or section?
- Does each paragraph have a distinct topic sentence?
- Do the subsequent sentences in this paragraph match this topic sentence?
- Do paragraphs connect logically with each other to create a flow?

A checklist such as this can also guide partnership work, where students swap essays to evaluate the structural clarity of each other's expository writing.

Once students have strengthened their paragraphs, you will also push them toward revising in ways that make the linkages between these paragraphs clear. You'll remind them of the use of transitions or linking words to connect one paragraph to the next. It may be easier to do this if writers focus on the topic sentence of each paragraph and decide how these topic sentences connect with each other. You'll also want students to evaluate their headings and subheadings and to see if more of these need to be created.

Teach students to consider the needs of their readers, as well as what they are trying to teach, when making revision decisions.

Then there are other revision questions: Does the reader have ample support to understand technical words (possibly from an explanation within the paragraph itself or through a text feature such as a glossary, sidebar, or footnote)? Would the text benefit from the addition of a text feature? If some of your students have returned to their angled All-About books, you may highlight pages of a great nonfiction book that uses diagrams with a zoomed-in image to teach the reader even more. Or, with a small group of students, you may point out how the author starts with the most important information first and then gives more specific details later on the page.

Sometimes, writers realize that the way they wrote something doesn't match what they really intended to say. In essay writing, this can happen if the thesis statement is not clear or is not supported throughout the essay. In other forms of informational writing, this can happen if the heading or subheading does not match the text that follows.

Essay writers may have new evidence to support their ideas from earlier in the year, or they may have shifted their thinking about the subject and need to modify their thesis.

BEND V: EDITING AND CELEBRATING

Allow students to reflect on their own editing needs across pieces, creating personal editing checklists.

Across the year, you've encouraged kids to give tricky words their best try and move on, to use spelling patterns from word study to spell tricky words, and to use the word wall to learn commonly misspelled high-frequency words. You've nudged kids to use big fancy vocabulary even when they aren't sure of the exact spelling, and you've been studying words during word study, read-aloud, and other times of the day.

Now is the time of year to bring it all together. Dust off all the old charts—if you've still got them—and teach kids to use them all, all the time. In this unit, you may want to teach kids that they can create their own personal editing checklists by looking across their own writing to notice the kinds of things for which they need reminders. Writers notice their own spelling challenges so that they can always be on the lookout. Anybody who writes knows his or her own weaknesses. Teach kids to search their writing to see if they are the kind of writer who misspells certain high-frequency words every time. Or maybe they are the kind of writer who always forgets a particular spelling pattern, or perhaps they forget to reread their writing to check it over. Teach kids that every writer has some habit, or even a bunch of habits or patterns in their writing. Finding those patterns and knowing to double-check for them is incredibly useful.

Celebrate the writing in the classroom, as well as the writers.

As the year and the unit wind down, you will want to take time to celebrate the extensive work that children have done during this month and across the year. You will want to take time to have children celebrate the work they have produced and the great strides they have made as writers. That is to say, you will want to hold a writing celebration that is about not only the writing but also the writers.

If you made photocopies of the original pieces that children revised, you might choose this time to take those pieces back out and put them side by side with the newest version. As children share the before and after pieces of writing, they can take their classmates on their journey of revision, sharing what made them decide to revise this particular piece, or these particular pieces, and how they chose to revise those pieces. Then too, writers might share how this process enhanced not only their work but themselves as writers.

Prompt students to think about carrying their writing work forward. Invite fourth-grade teachers to share in the celebration.

Many times our children leave our classrooms strong and energetic writers and then return from summer break the following September out of practice and out of passion. Since it is likely that this will be the last writing unit of the year, you may want to spend some time helping the kids make plans for how they will take all they've learned with them into *next year's* writing workshop. You might ask children to write a reflection, sharing what they learned and how they have grown. This reflection, accompanied by the original works, drafts created during revision, and the published pieces, can travel with them into next year's classrooms. Next year's teachers might even begin their writing workshop with children sharing their body of revised work and all that they know about writing with the class as a way of building a writing community and learning about the children in their room.

Then, too, you might choose to invite next year's teachers to your classroom during this time to acquaint themselves with the students with whom they will work in the next grade level. These teachers might join your class for a writing workshop and watch your students engaged in the process. The teachers can talk with your children about their process and their pieces. The students might study the teachers' notebooks and folders. The teachers might also join the celebration, partaking in the end of year reflection. Listening to your kids share all that they know about writing will help those teachers to plan units of study that build on the work you and your students have done.

THERE IS NO GREATER CHALLENGE, WHEN TEACHING WRITING, than to learn to confer well. And conferring well is a big deal. It matters. If you can pull your chair alongside a child, study what he or she has been doing, listen to the child's own plans, and then figure out a way to spur that youngster on to greater heights, that ability will allow you to generate minilessons, mid-workshop teaching points, and share sessions that have real-world traction.

However, knowing conferring matters doesn't make it easier to master. Even if you know that learning to confer well is important, even if you devote yourself to reading about the art of conferring, you are apt to feel ill prepared for the challenges that you encounter.

I remember Alexandra, tall with long brown hair and a thick Russian accent. I'd pull up beside her after the minilesson, notebook in hand, ready to execute the perfect conference. We'd talk, I'd research, and without fail, every time, I'd be left with the same terrifying realization: "She's already doing everything! I don't know *what* to teach her." In an attempt to preserve my own integrity, I'd leave her with a compliment. Despite having joined our class midyear, despite the challenge of mastering a new language and adapting to a new culture, Alexandra implemented anything and everything I hoped she would as a writer. I thought, "What should she do next?" I was stuck.

Then there was a child I'll call Matthew, who in truth represents many others across my years as a teacher. It felt as if I was always conferring with him—modeling, pulling him into small groups, implementing all the scaffolds I knew of—and yet he didn't make the progress I hoped for. In reality, it felt like nothing worked. As I'd sit beside him, looking over his work, I couldn't help but wonder what was happening. Why was my teaching passing him over? What do I teach him, right now in this conference, when his writing needs *everything*?

If you have had conferences like these and ended up wondering what's wrong, know that you aren't alone. Teachers across the world find that conferring well is a challenge. Most of us have, at one time or another, written questions on our hands, or on cue cards, that we want to remember to ask. Many of us have mantras that we repeat to ourselves, over and over. "Teach the writer, not the writing." "It's a good conference if the writer leaves wanting to write." "Your job is to let this child teach you how to help."

Many of the books on conferring will help you understand the architecture of a conference. You'll learn to research first, then to compliment, then to give critical feedback and/or to teach. You'll learn tips about each part of a conference. When researching, follow more than one line of inquiry. If you ask, "What are you working on?" and hear about the child's concerns with one part of the writing, don't jump to teaching that part of the writing until you generate a second line of inquiry—whether it's "What do you plan to do next?" or "How do you feel about this piece?" or "If you were going to revise this, what might you do?" There are similar tips that you'll learn about other aspects of conferring too.

But you will no doubt feel as if there is another kind of help that you need. You will probably want help knowing not only *how* to confer, but also knowing *what* to teach.

Visiting hundreds of schools has given me a unique perspective on that question, a perspective that may be difficult to come by when you are in one classroom, with one set of children with very particular needs. After working in so many schools, with so many youngsters, I've begun to see patterns. I notice that when

X is taught, children often need Y or Z. I meet one Matthew in Chicago and another in Tulsa, Oklahoma. I meet Alexandras in Seattle and Shanghai. And I've begun to realize that, despite the uniqueness of each child, there are familiar ways they struggle and predictable ways in which a teacher can help with those struggles. Those ways of helping come from using all we know about learning progressions, writing craft, language development, and grade-specific standards to anticipate and plan for the individualized instruction that students are apt to need.

The charts that follow are designed to help you feel less empty-handed when you confer. I've anticipated some of the most common struggles you will see as you teach narrative, opinion, and information writing through the units of study in this series and I've named a bit about those struggles in the "If . . ." column of the charts. When you identify a child (or a group of children) who resembles the "If . . ." that I describe, then see if perhaps the strategy I suggest might help. That strategy is described in the column titled "After acknowledging what the child is doing well, you might say. . . ." Of course, you will want to use your own language. What I've presented is just one way your teaching might go!

Often you will want to leave the writer with a tangible artifact of your work together. This will ensure that he or she remembers the strategy you've worked on and next time you meet with the child, it will allow you to look back and see what you taught the last time you worked together. It will be important for you to follow up on whatever the work is that you and the youngster decide upon together. Plan to check back in, asking a quick "How has the work we talked about been going for you? Can you show me where you've tried it?"

Some teachers choose to print the "Leave the writer with . . ." column onto reams of stickers or label paper (so they can be easily placed in students' notebooks). You also might choose to print them out on plain paper and tape them onto the writer's desk as a reminder (see the CD-ROM for this chart in reproducible format). I hope these charts will help you anticipate, spot, and teach into the challenges your writers face during the independent work portion of your writing workshop.

Narrative Writing

If . . .	After acknowledging what the child is doing well, you might say . . .	Leave the writer with . . .
Structure and Cohesion		
The story lacks focus. This writer has written a version of a "bed to bed" story, beginning with the start of a day or large event ("I woke up and had breakfast") and progressing to the end ("I came home. It was a great day"). The event unfolds in a bit-by-bit fashion, with each part of the story receiving equal weight.	You are learning to write more and more, stretching your stories across tons of pages. That's great. But here's the new challenge. Writers need to be able to write a lot and still write a *focused* story. What I mean by this is that writers can write a whole story that only lasts twenty minutes, and it can still be tons of pages long. To write a really fleshed-out, well-developed Small Moment story, it is important to move more slowly through the sequence of the event, and capture the details on the page.	Not the whole trip, the whole day: twenty minutes! Write with details. I said, I thought, I did.
The story is confusing or seems to be missing important information. This writer has written a story that leaves you lost, unable to picture the moment or understand the full sequence of events. She may have left out information regarding where she was or why something was happening, or may have switched suddenly to a new part of the story without alerting the reader.	I really want to understand this story, but it gets confusing for me. Will you remember that writers need to become readers and to reread their own writing, asking, "Does this make sense? Have I left anything out that my reader might need to know?" Sometimes it is helpful to ask a partner to read your story, as well, and to tell you when the story is making sense (thumbs up) and when it is confusing (thumbs down).	I reread my writing to make it clearer. I ask myself, "Does this make sense? Have I left anything out that my reader might need to know?" If I need to, I add more information or a part that is missing into the story.
The story has no tension. This writer's story is flat, without any sense of conflict or tension. The story is more of a chronicle than a story. If there is a problem, there is no build-up around possible solutions. Instead, the dog is simply lost and then found.	You told what happened in your story, in order, so I get it. But to make this into the kind of story that readers can't put down, the kind that readers read by flashlight in bed, you have to add what writers call *edge-of-the-seat tension*. Instead of just saying *I did this, I did this, I did this,* you need to have the narrator want something really badly and then run into difficulties, or trouble . . . so readers are thinking, "Will it work? Won't it?" You've got to get readers all wound up! Right now, reread and find the part of the story where you could show what the main character really wants.	Edge-of-the-seat tension: • Someone who really wants something. • Someone encounters trouble. • Someone tries, tries, tries.

If . . .	After acknowledging what the child is doing well, you might say . . .	Leave the writer with . . .

The story has no real or significant ending.
 	
This writer has ended his story in a way that feels disappointing to the reader. Occasionally this happens because he has left loose ends unresolved, but most often it is because the ending of the story has little to do with the significance of the story itself. The ending may be something like, "Then I went home," or "The End!" He needs help identifying what his story is really about and then crafting an ending that ties directly to that meaning.
	Sometimes it seems like your endings just trail off, and they aren't as powerful as they could be because of that. Writers know that the ending of a story is the last thing with which a reader will be left. Today, I want to teach you one tip for writing an ending that is particularly powerful. Writers ask, "What is this story really about?" Once they have the answer to that, they decide on a bit of dialogue or internal thinking, a descriptive detail, or a small action that will end the story in a way that ties back to that meaning.	Writers end a story in a way that shows what the story is *really* about. They might do this by including:
		• Dialogue
		   • Internal thinking
		   • A descriptive detail
		   • A small action that ties back to the true meaning behind the story

The writer is new to the writing workshop or this particular genre of writing. This writer struggles because narrative is a new genre for her. She may display certain skill sets (e.g., the ability to use beautifully descriptive language or literary devices) but lacks the vision of what she is being asked to produce. Her story is probably long and unfocused and is usually dominated by summary, not storytelling.	Someone famously once said, "You can't hit a target if you don't know what that target is." This is especially true for writers. They can't write well if they don't have a vision, a mental picture, of what they hope to produce. Today, I want to teach you that one way writers learn about the kinds of writing they hope to produce is by studying mentor texts. They read a mentor text once, enjoying it as a story. Then, they read it again, this time asking, "How does this kind of story seem to go?" They label what they notice and then try it in their own writing.	Writers use mentor texts to help them imagine what they hope to write. They: • Read the text and enjoy it as a good story. • Reread the text and ask, "How does this kind of story seem to go?" • Note what they notice. • Try to do some of what they noticed in their own writing.
The writer does not use paragraphs. This writer does not use paragraphs to separate the different parts of his story. Because of this, the story is difficult to read and hold on to. He needs support understanding the importance of paragraphs, as well as the various ways writers use them.	Your writing will be a thousand times easier to read when you start using paragraphs. A paragraph is like a signal to a reader. It says, "Halt! Take a tiny break. Do you understand what is happening so far? Okay, I'm going to keep going!" Paragraphs give your readers an opportunity to take in your stories, and they also alert readers to important things like scene changes and new dialogue. Today, I want to teach you a few of the ways writers use paragraphs. Writers use paragraphs when a new event is starting, when their story is switching to a new time or place, when a new character speaks, or to separate out an important part that needs space around it.	Make a new paragraph here: • Very important part that needs space around it • New event • New time • New place • New character speaks

If . . .	After acknowledging what the child is doing well, you might say . . .	Leave the writer with . . .
Elaboration		
The writer has created a story that is sparse, with little elaboration. This writer has written a story that is short, with one or more parts that need elaboration. She has conveyed the main outline of an event (this happened, then this happened, then this happened), but there is no sense that she has expanded on any one particular part.	You have gotten skilled at telling what happens, in order, but you write with just the bare-bones sequence. Like, if you went out for supper yesterday and I asked you, "How was your dinner at the restaurant?" And you answered, "I went to the restaurant. I ate food. It was good." That's not the best story, right? It is just the bare bones with no flesh on them—like a skeleton. Can you try to flesh your story out?	Not: I ate food. I came home. But: Details, details, details or: Not:
The story is riddled with details. In an attempt to elaborate or make a story compelling, the writer has listed what seem to be an endless number of tangential details. ("I got on the ride. There were a lot of people there. I was wearing a bright red shirt with a little giraffe on it. I was eating funnel cake.") This sort of elaboration often makes the piece feel monotonous, as if there is no real purpose guiding the writer's choice of details.	Although you are great at including details, you actually choose too many details. Writers are choosy about the details they include in a story. They know they can't include every detail they remember, so they have to decide which parts of their story to stretch out with details and which parts to move through more quickly. Writers ask, "What is this story really about?" and then stretch out the part of the story that goes with that meaning. Then, they cut details from the parts that are less important.	Although it is great to write with details, some writers write with too many details. Writers need to decide which details to *keep* and which to *cut*: • They ask, "What is my story really about?" • They stretch out the heart of the story. • They shorten less important parts.
The story is swamped with dialogue. This writer is attempting to story-tell, not summarize, but is relying too heavily on dialogue to accomplish this mission. The story is full of endless dialogue ("Let's play at the park," I said. "Okay," Jill said. "Maybe we should play on the swings," I said. "I agree," Jill said. "Great!" I said). This writer needs to learn that dialogue is an important part of storytelling but cannot be the only device a writer uses to move a story forward.	Sometimes, writers make their characters talk—and talk and talk and talk. Today, I want to teach you that writers use dialogue, but they use it sparingly. They make sure their writing has a balance of action and dialogue by alternating between the two and by cutting dialogue that does not give the reader important information about the character or the story.	Writers make sure that their writing has a balance of dialogue and action: • They often alternate between action and dialogue as they write. • They cut dialogue that does not give the reader important information about the character or story.

If . . .	After acknowledging what the child is doing well, you might say . . .	Leave the writer with . . .
The writer has written the external story but not the internal story. This writer has captured the events of a story precisely, and likely has done a fine job of moving the story along at an appropriate pace. What is missing, however, is the internal story. That is, as each event occurs the main character is merely swept along with the current of events ("'Don't you ever do that again!' my dad yelled. He wagged his finger at me. I went up to my room and sat down to do my homework") and has little emotional response. The reader is left wondering what the main character is feeling and thinking throughout the story, and as a result, the story lacks a certain depth.	When we first learn to write stories, we learn to tell the events that happened. We tell what happened first, then next, then next. As we become strong writers, though, it's important not just to write the external story, but also to write the internal story, as well. Today, I want to teach you that when planning for and drafting a story, the writer plans not just the actions, but also the character's *reactions* to the events.	Writers tell not just what happened in a story—the *actions*—but also how the character felt about each of those events—the *reactions*.
The writer struggles to identify and convey a deeper meaning. This writer's story likely contains most of the surface elements you are looking for but seems to lack a sense of purpose. When asked why he is writing this particular piece or what he hopes to convey to his reader, he struggles to find an answer. Because of this, each part of the story is often given equal attention, without any one part having been elaborated on. Dialogue, details, and other forms of narrative craft are used to move the story forward but do not contribute to the reader's understanding of the meaning or theme.	Everybody has stories to tell. At a certain point in your life as a writer, knowing *why* you want to tell these stories becomes almost as important as writing them. What I mean by this, and what I want to teach you today, is that writers reflect on the moments of their lives and ask, "What is this story really about? What do I want my reader to know about me?" Then, they use all they know about narrative craft to bring that meaning forward.	Writers ask: • What is this story really about? • What do I want my reader to know about me? Then they use all they know about narrative craft to bring that meaning forward.
The writer is ready to use literary devices. This writer is successfully using a variety of narrative techniques and would benefit from learning to use literary devices. She has a clear sense of the meaning behind his story, as well as the places where this meaning might be emphasized or further revealed.	I think you are ready for a new challenge. When writers are strong—using all sorts of craft, writing focused, well-paced stories—it often signals that they are ready for something new. I've noticed that you are trying to bring out what your story is really about and want to teach you one way that writers do this: using literary devices. Writers use comparisons (like metaphors and similes), repetition, and even symbols to highlight important messages in stories.	Literary devices writers use to reveal meaning to a reader: • Metaphors and similes • Repetition • Symbolism

If . . .	After acknowledging what the child is doing well, you might say . . .	Leave the writer with . . .
The writer summarizes rather than story-tells. There is probably a sense that this writer is disconnected from the series of events—listing what happened first, then next, then next. He writes predominately by overviewing what happened ("On the way to school I was almost attacked by a dog but I got there okay"). The writer rarely uses dialogue, descriptive details, or other forms of narrative craft to convey the story to his reader.	Writers don't take huge steps through their experience, writing like this: "I had an argument. Then I went to bed." Instead, writers take tiny steps, writing more like this, "'It was your turn!' I yelled and then I turned and walked out of the room really fast. I slammed the door and went to my bedroom. I was so furious that I just sat on my bed for a long time." It helps to show what happened rather than just telling the main gist of it.	Not giant steps, but baby steps. Show, not tell.
Language		
The writer struggles with spelling. This writer's piece is riddled with spelling mistakes. This does not necessarily mean the writing is not strong (in fact, the story may be very strong), but the spelling mistakes compromise the reader's ability to understand it. The writer's struggle with spelling may stem from various places—difficulty understanding and applying spelling patterns, a limited stock of high-frequency words, lack of investment, the acquisition of English as a new language—and diagnosing the underlying problem will be an important precursor to teaching into it.	One of the things I'm noticing about your writing is how beautiful it sounds when you read it aloud. I looked more closely, curious about how I had missed all the beauty you've captured on this page, and realized that all your spelling mistakes make it difficult for me (and probably other readers, too) to understand. Today, I want to teach you a few techniques writers use to help them spell. Writers use the classroom word wall, they stretch words out and write down the sounds they hear, and they use words they *do* know how to spell to help them with those they don't know how to spell.	Writers work hard at their spelling. They: • Use the **word wall**. • **S-T-R-E-T-C-H** words out and write down the sounds they hear. • Use words they *know* (*found*) to help them spell words they *don't know* (*compound, round*).
The writer struggles with end punctuation. This story amounts to what appears to be one long, endless sentence. The writer may have distinct sentences ("We ran down the road James was chasing us we thought we needed to run faster to escape him") that are simply not punctuated. Alternatively, she may have strung her sentences together using an endless number of *and*s, *then*s, and *but*s in an attempt at cohesion. ("We ran down the road and James was chasing us and we thought that we needed to run faster to escape him but then we could hear his footsteps and his breathing and we were scared").	I read your piece today, and it sounded a bit like this. "We ran down the road and James was chasing us and we thought that we needed to run faster to escape him but then we could hear his footsteps and his breathing and we were scared." Phew, I was out of breath! Today, I want to teach you that writers use end punctuation to give their readers a little break, to let them take a breath, before moving onto the next thing that happened in the story. One way to figure out where to put end punctuation is to reread your piece aloud, notice where you find yourself stopping to take a small breath, and put a period, exclamation point, or question mark there.	Writers reread their pieces aloud, notice where readers should stop and take a small breath because one thought has ended, and use end punctuation to help mark those places.

If . . .	After acknowledging what the child is doing well, you might say . . .	Leave the writer with . . .
The Process of Generating Ideas		
The writer has "nothing to write about." This writer often leaves the minilesson, returns to his seat, and sits idly, waiting for you to visit. When you do visit, he is generally quick to tell you that he has "nothing to write about." This writer needs help with independence, but also with understanding that life is one big source of stories. As long as one is living, one has something to write about!	I'm noticing that you often have trouble finding things to write about and I wanted to remind you that life is one big source of story ideas. Writers see the world through special eyes, imagining stories in the tiniest of moments. Writers find stories at the dinner table, while walking down the street, in the classroom, and at recess. Writers know that it matters less *what* they write about and more *how* they write about it.	Writers have the eyes to find stories everywhere. They know it matters less *what* they write about and more *how* they write about it.
The writer's notebook work does not represent all he can do. This writer is content to summarize and write in cursory ways in her notebook, and does not hold herself to using all she knows when collecting entries. This may mean the entries are short, underdeveloped, or lack narrative craft. When you look at this child's entries, you do not get the sense that she is working to do her best work while collecting.	Many people think that the writer's notebook is just a place to collect stuff and that real writing happens when you pick a seed idea and draft on lined paper. I sort of get the idea you think that way. It is true that the notebook is a place for collecting, but it is also true that the notebook is a place for *practicing*. Today, I want to teach you that writers hold themselves accountable to using everything they know about good writing whenever they write, even in the notebook. This includes everything they know about structure, storytelling, revision, and editing!	Writers use their notebooks to practice becoming better writers. They use everything they know about structure, storytelling, and even revision and editing!
The Process of Drafting		
The writer has trouble maintaining stamina and volume. This writer has a hard time putting words down on the page. It may be that he writes for a long period of time producing very little or that he refuses to write for longer than a few minutes. The writer often has avoidance behaviors (e.g., trips to the bathroom during writing workshop, a pencil tip that breaks repeatedly). He gets very little writing done during the workshop, despite urging from you.	Today, I want to teach you a little trick that often works for me when I'm having trouble staying focused. When writing is hard for me, I set small, manageable goals for myself. I make sure these goals are something I *know* I can do, like writing for ten minutes straight. Then, when I reach my goal, I give myself a little gift, like a short walk or a few minutes to sketch a picture. Then, I get back to writing again.	Writers set goals for themselves and work hard to achieve them. When they do, they reward themselves for their hard work.

If . . .	After acknowledging what the child is doing well, you might say . . .	Leave the writer with . . .
The writer struggles to work independently. This student is often at your side, asking questions or needing advice. She struggles to write on her own and only seems to generate ideas when you are sitting beside her. When she does write, she needs constant "checks" and accolades. She is task-oriented. That is, she will complete one thing you have taught her to do and then sit and wait to be told what to do next. She does not rely on charts or other materials to keep her going.	As a writer, it is important that you take control of your own writing life. You can't be content to sit back and relax. Instead, you have to ask yourself, "What in this room might help me get back on track as a writer?" Then, you use those resources to get started again. You can look at charts in the room, ask your partner for help, read mentor texts for inspiration, or even look back over old writing for new ideas. or One thing I'm noticing about you as a writer is that you write with me in mind. What I mean by this is that when I teach something, you try it. When I suggest something, you try it. But I am not the only writing teacher in this room. Believe it or not, *you* can be your own writing teacher, too. Today, I want to teach you how to look at your own work against a checklist, assess for what is going well and what you might do better, and then set goals for how you might revise your current piece and for what you might try out in your future work too.	When you are stuck, you can: • Consult charts. • Ask your partner for help. • Read mentor texts for inspiration. • Look back over old writing for new ideas.
The Process of Revision		
The writer does not have personal goals for her writing progress. If you ask, "What are you working on?" this writer acts surprised. "My writing," he says, and indeed, you are pretty sure that is what he is doing. He is trying to crank out the required amount of text. He doesn't have more specific goals about how to do things better that are influencing him.	Can I ask you something? Who is the boss of your writing? I'm asking that because you need to be the boss of your writing, and to be the best boss you can be, you need to give yourself little assignments. You need to take yourself by the hand and say, "From now on, you should be working on this," and then after a bit, "Now you should be working on this."	My Writing Goals Are: 1. _____ 2. _____ 3. _____
The Process of Editing		
The writer does not use what he knows about editing while writing. This writer is not applying what she knows about spelling, grammar, and punctuation while writing. You may notice that you have taught a particular spelling pattern, she mastered it in isolation, but she is not using that knowledge during writing workshop. She may also spell word wall words wrong or misspell words that are similar (e.g., spelling *getting* correctly but misspelling *setting*). This writer needs to be reminded that editing is not something left for the last stages of writing. Instead, writers use all they know *as they write*.	You are the boss of your own writing, and part of being the boss is making sure that you are doing, and using, everything you know while you write. Often when people think of editing, they think of it as something they do just before publishing. This is true, but it is also true that writers edit as they write. Today, I want to teach you that writers use an editing checklist to remind them of what they've learned about spelling, punctuation, and grammar. They take a bit of time each day to make sure they are using all they know as they write.	Editing Checklist • Read, asking, "Will this make sense to a stranger?" • Check the punctuation. • Do your words look like they are spelled correctly?

Information Writing

If . . .	After acknowledging what the child is doing well, you might say . . .	Leave the writer with . . .
Structure and Cohesion		
The writer has not established a clear organization for his book. This writer is struggling with organization. It is likely that his book is a jumble of information about a larger topic, with no clear subheadings or internal organization. The writer may have a table of contents but the chapters actually contain a whole bunch of stuff unrelated to the chapter titles or the writer may have skipped this part of the process all together.	One of the most important things information writers do is organize their writing. Making chapters or headings is one way to make it easier for your readers to learn about your topic. It's like creating little signs that say, "Hey, reader, I'm about to start talking about a new part of my topic!" It helps to name what the upcoming part of your writing will be about and then to write about just that thing. When information writers notice they are about to start writing about something new, they often create a new heading that tells the reader what the next part will be about.	One thing About that thing About that thing About that thing Another thing About that next thing About that next thing ~~Something else~~ ~~Something else~~ Another thing Not: One thing Another thing The first thing A whole other thing

If . . .	After acknowledging what the child is doing well, you might say . . .	Leave the writer with . . .
Information overlaps in various sections. This writer attempted to organize his piece, but has various sections that overlap. The writer may have repeated similar information in several parts of his piece or may have attempted to give the same information worded differently. Often he has sections and subsections that are too closely related and therefore struggles to find different information for different parts.	It is great that you have a system for organizing things. It is sort of like this page is a drawer and you just put things about (XYZ) in it. And this chapter is a drawer and you just put stuff about (ABC) in it. There are a few mess-ups—places where you have some whole other things scattered in, or some things that are in two places. That always happens. You got to expect it. So what writers do is just what you have done. They write organized pieces. But then, when they are done writing, they . . . Do you know? They reread to check. Just like you can reread to check your spelling, you can reread to check that the right things are in the right drawers, the right sections.	Writers reread to check that things are in the right drawers.
The writer is ready to experiment with alternative structures of organization. This writer may have a relatively strong organizational structure to her information piece, but you sense there are better options or more challenging avenues she might take. Then too, she may have tried to organize her piece one way, but the topic does not lend itself well to the structure she has chosen. In either instance, she is ready to broaden her repertoire in regard to organizational structure and study mentor texts to imagine the alternate ways her text might go.	One of the greatest things about information writing is that there are so many different ways a text can go. If we were to lay out a few different books on the same topic, we would find dozens of different ways the authors chose to organize them. Some authors, like Gail Gibbons, write chronologically, others write about different sections of a topic, and some authors use pros and cons or questions and answers to organize their information. The options are endless! When writers are looking to challenge themselves and try out some new ways of organizing their writing, they study mentor texts. One way to study an information text is to read asking, "How does this author structure and organize his information?" Then, you can try out the same structure with your own writing.	Information writers study mentor texts and ask, "How does this author structure and organize his information?" Then, they try the same with their own writing.
The writer has chosen a topic that is too broad. This writer has chosen a topic that is broad, such as dogs or the Civil War, and has likely created a table of contents that suggests the product will be more of an all-about book. In an attempt to make his writing more sophisticated, and the process of crafting an information piece more demanding, you will want to teach him to narrow his topic a bit.	I was looking at your topic choice earlier and thought to myself, "He is ready for a challenge!" You chose a topic that is very broad, very big. There is nothing wrong with that. In fact, it means you'll have a lot to say! But when information writers want to push themselves, when they want to craft a text that is more sophisticated, they narrow their topic. Today, I'm going to teach you how to narrow your topic by asking, "What is *one part* of this subject I can write a lot about?"	Writers challenge themselves by narrowing their topics. They ask, "What is *one part* of this subject I can write a lot about?"

If . . .	After acknowledging what the child is doing well, you might say . . .	Leave the writer with . . .
The piece is lacking an introduction and/or conclusion. This writer has written an information piece that is missing an introduction and/or conclusion. Alternatively, it may be that the writer attempted to introduce and then conclude her piece but did so in overly folksy or ineffective ways. (For instance, she might have begun, "My name is Michelle and I'm going to teach you everything you want to know about sharks. They are really cool." Later, she'll likely end along the same lines: "That's everything about sharks! I hope you learned a lot!") She is ready to adopt a more sophisticated tone and learn more nuanced (and subtle) ways of pulling readers in and providing closure.	In stories, writers use introductions to pull our readers in. Their conclusions, or endings, usually give the reader some closure. Information writing isn't really much different. Writers use introductions to *pull* readers in, often by giving them a little information on the topic (orienting them). Then, they give their reader a sense of closure by wrapping things up with a conclusion (sometimes restating some key points about the topic) and leaving the reader with something to think about.	Introductions pull readers in: • Give a bit of information about the topic. Orient your reader. Conclusions give readers closure and wrap things up: • Restate a bit about the topic. • Leave your reader with something to think about.
Elaboration		
Each section is short and needs to be elaborated on. This writer has attempted to group his information, but each section is short. For example, he may have listed one or two facts related to a specific subsection but he is stuck at what to add next.	Information writers need to be able to say a lot about each part of their topic, or to elaborate. There are a few things you can do to make each part of your book chock-full of information. One thing that helps is to write in partner sentences. This means that instead of writing one sentence about each thing, you can push yourself to write two sentences (or more) about each thing. So if I said, "George sits at a desk when he is at school" and I wanted to write with partner sentences, what else might I say about George sitting at his desk? You are right. It can help to fill in stuff about why, kinds of, where, how many, and so on. A whole other thing you can do to get yourself to say more is use prompts like "It's also important to know this because . . ."; "Also . . ."; and "What this means is. . . ."	Writers Elaborate 1. They check to make sure they have at least four or five pieces of information for each subtopic. If not, they consider cutting that section and starting a new one. 2. Writers elaborate by creating partner sentences. 3. They use prompts like "It's also important to know . . ."; "Also . . ."; and "What this means is . . ." to say more about a particular piece of information.

If . . .	After acknowledging what the child is doing well, you might say . . .	Leave the writer with . . .
The writer elaborates by adding fact upon fact. This writer has elaborated but has done so by adding fact upon fact upon fact. As a result, her writing reads like a list rather than a cohesive section of text. This writer would benefit from learning to add a bit of her own voice into her writing, relying not just on factual information but on her own ability to synthesize and make sense of these facts for the reader.	You have tackled the first step in information writing—gathering the information needed to support various subtopics. Here's the thing, though. Writers don't *just* list facts for readers. It is also their job to take these facts and make something of them, to help explain why they are important to the reader. Writers often use prompts like "In other words . . . ," "What this really means is . . . ," "This shows . . . ," and "All of this is important because . . ." to help readers understand the information they've put forth.	Information writers don't just list fact after fact. They *spice up* their writing by adding a bit of their own voice: • "In other words . . ." • "What this really means is . . ." • "This shows . . ." • "All of this is important because . . ."
The writer goes off on tangents when elaborating. This writer has tried to elaborate on information but tends to get into personal and tangential details ("Dogs really are great pets. I have a dog, too. I had a cat too but she peed on the counter so my Dad got rid of her"). Or by repeating the same information again and again. Or by being chit-chatty ("And I love *love* that and think it is really funny, so *so* funny").	You are working hard to say a lot about your topic, aren't you? I have to give you a tip, though. Sometimes, in your hard work to say a lot, you are doing things that don't really work that well. Let me give you an example of things that don't work when writers are writing information books, and will you see if you do those things some of the time? Pretend I was writing about dogs, so I wrote that there are many kinds of dogs, and the kinds of dogs are divided into groups, like spaniels, retrievers, toy dogs, and so forth. If I then said, "And I have a dog and a cat too and the cat's name is Barney . . . ," would that go in my report? You are right. It wouldn't go because it isn't really teaching information and ideas about the topic—and it might not even be about the topic. If I wrote "And I love, love, *love* dogs," would that go? And if I said, "Some dogs are spaniels, some are retrievers," would that go? You see, there are things people do when they are trying to elaborate, to say more, that just don't work that well. So what writers do is they cross them out and try other ways to elaborate. You will want to reread your writing and to have the courage to say no sometimes. Or: Today, I want to teach you that information writers revise by checking to make sure all their information is important and new. They cut out parts where they started to talk about their own life too much and got off topic, parts where they included information that doesn't go with what they were writing about, or parts where they repeat the same thing more than once.	Information writers cut parts where: • They started talking about their life too much and got off topic. • They included information that doesn't fit with what the rest of the paragraph is about. • They repeated something they'd already written.

If . . .	After acknowledging what the child is doing well, you might say . . .	Leave the writer with . . .
The writer does not elaborate on information from outside sources. The writer has included information from outside sources, such as quotes, facts, or statistics, but does not elaborate on this information for his reader. As a result, his writing is often very short and hops from interesting fact to interesting fact.	I love all the research you have included in your information piece. It really shows that you are an expert on this topic. One way to show you are an expert, to show all you know about your topic, is by including outside information like quotes, facts, and statistics. Another way to be an expert and teach your readers (the way I'm going to teach you today) is by elaborating on those facts. Today, I want to teach you that writers don't just plop information into their writing. Instead, they explain what it means to their readers by using phrases like "What this means is . . ." or "In other words. . . ."	Writers don't just plop information into their writing. Instead, they explain what it means to their readers by using phrases like "What this means is . . ." or "In other words. . . ."
Language		
The writer incorporates quotes, facts, and statistics but does so awkwardly. This writer uses quotes, facts, statistics, and other outside information to elaborate on the sections of her information text. The information is well organized, and the facts and quotes are generally well placed but often sound awkward. It is not clear that the writer understands how to move from her words to the words and examples of an author or experts, and she needs help with ways to do this more fluently.	Quotes, facts, and statistics are incredibly important in information writing, because they tell a reader that, yes, I have done my research and know a lot about my topic! Today, I want to teach you how to take quotes, facts, and statistics and make them sound like a part of your writing. You can do this by using transitional phrases like *for instance*, *one example*, or *according to*.	Writers use transitional phrases to introduce quotes, facts, and statistics. Example: Sharks aren't that dangerous. One example of this is basking sharks. People in the Hamptons often see them and they are slow moving and harmless. According to Science-Facts.com, "more people die of alligator attacks than shark attacks."
Transitions from section to section sound awkward. This writer has organized his information piece into sections and paragraphs, but the transitions from part to part feel awkward. He would benefit from a few tips aimed at helping him ease readers into each new section of his text.	One of the hardest parts about being an information writer is moving from one part of a topic to the next. One second a writer is talking about the Lewis and Clark expedition, and the next second he is talking about the Louisiana Purchase. In his mind he knows how these two things connect (they are both about westward expansion), but this isn't always clear to his readers. Today, I want to teach you how to write a topic sentence that reminds readers what your big topic is and introduces them to what your next section will be about. One way writers do this is by connecting each section back to the larger topic.	Information writers use topic sentences to say what a section will be about and explain how it relates to the big, overall topic. Example: Lewis and Clark were famous explorers who took on a daring adventure. They were an important part of westward expansion. or Another important part of westward expansion was the Louisiana Purchase, because it gave Americans new land to explore and settle.

If . . .	After acknowledging what the child is doing well, you might say . . .	Leave the writer with . . .
The writer does not incorporate domain-specific vocabulary. This writer has written about a topic but has done so without incorporating domain-specific vocabulary. It may be that the child simply glossed over using terms such as *caravan* or *brigade* (because she did not understand them or know how to incorporate them into her own writing) or used simpler language in place of complex vocabulary.	As an information writer, it's important that you come across as an expert on your topic. Readers expect to learn something new, and one way to teach them something new is by using technical, expert vocabulary. Today, I want to teach you that writers don't just toss these words into their writing, though. Instead, they learn what they mean, and then they define them for their readers. They can either use the word and then give its definition, or tuck the word's definition into a sentence using commas.	Information writers use expert vocabulary (and define it for their readers, too). They can: • Use the word and then explain what it means. Example: Loyalists were people who remained loyal to the king during the American Revolution. • Tuck the definition into the sentence using two commas. Example: Loyalists, people who remained loyal to the king during the American Revolution, fought throughout the war.
The Process of Generating Ideas		
The writer chooses topics about which he has little expertise and/or that are difficult to research. This child often generates ideas quickly, and they often relate to his passions. He might decide to write about the melting of the polar ice caps and its effect on seals, during a unit in which students are writing about areas of personal expertise. Or his access to research material on that topic is limited and is difficult to comprehend. This child needs help mining his life for topics that are closer to home and assessing his own ability to write long, strong, and focused about a particular topic.	Writers ask themselves some tough questions when they are choosing a topic for information writing. They ask : 1. Do I care about this topic? (You are already doing this!) 2. Do I know enough to imagine a possible table of contents? 3. Do I know one or two resources I can use to gather more information? If not, they pick a different topic.	When choosing a topic, information writers ask: • Do I care about this topic? • Do I know enough to imagine a possible table of contents? • Do I know one or two resources I can use to gather more information?
The writer simply copies facts into her notebook. This writer's "collecting" amounts to copying facts from books into her notebook. She copies lines verbatim, rarely bothering to paraphrase or quote. It may seem as if the child is not being overly discriminatory about what to include. That is, if the book says it, she writes it. In this way the child's notebook becomes an endless list of facts about a topic or, if the child has created organized categories, parts of a topic.	Research is a pretty hard thing to do as a writer. Researchers have a difficult job: They have to take the information that other people have written, sort through it, and then put it into their own words or quote it. You can't just copy what other authors have written into your notebook, because that would be stealing their words! Today, I want to teach you one way that writers take information from a book and incorporate it into their own writing. It's called *paraphrasing*. To paraphrase (or put something into your own words), it helps to read a chunk of text, close the book, say back an important part of what you just read, and then write it down in your own words.	One way researchers put information into their own words is by paraphrasing. They: 1. Read a chunk of the text. 2. Close the book. 3. Say back an important part of what they just read. 4. Write it down in their own words.

If . . .	After acknowledging what the child is doing well, you might say . . .	Leave the writer with . . .
The Process of Drafting		
The first draft is not organized. This writer has written a first draft that is disorganized. It may be that there is an underlying organizational structure (e.g., the writer grouped similar information together), but he did not use new pages, section titles, or transitions to let the reader in on this structure. Alternatively, the writer may have simply "written a draft," compiling all the information he collected into one ongoing piece of writing.	One of the most important things information writers do is organize. It can be hard for a reader to learn a lot of new information about, say, sharks. But when a writer organizes the information into sections, then it becomes easier for the reader to take it in. The reader knows that one part will be about sharks' bodies, another will be about what they eat, and another will be about their family life. As a writer, it's important to look at your draft and make sure that you've organized it in a way that will make sense to the reader. This usually means taking all the information or facts about one part of a topic (like sharks' bodies) and putting that together. Then, taking all the information about another topic (like what sharks eat) and putting that together. Then using section headings to make it clear what each part is about.	Information writers organize their writing! • Divide your topic into sections (you may have already done this while planning). • Put the information about one section together with a heading. • Put the information about another section together with a heading. • And so on . . . (Sometimes it helps to cut up your draft and tape different parts together!)
The Process of Revision		
The writer is "done" before revising. This writer is perfectly pleased with her first draft and declares, "I'm done" soon after completing it. Your revision minilessons do little to help inspire this writer to revise, and you feel you must constantly sit by her side and point out parts to revise for her to do the work.	I've noticed that you often have trouble thinking of ways to revise your piece. You write a draft and then it feels done. Sometimes when it is hard to come up with ideas for improving your writing, it helps to have a published writer help. You just look at a published book that you love and notice cool things that the author has done, then you revise to do those same things in your writing.	When writers feel done, they study a few mentor texts asking, "What has this writer done that I could try as well?"
The writer does not have a large repertoire of strategies to draw from. This writer lives off of each day's minilesson. He is task-oriented and generally applies (or attempts to apply) what you teach each day. This student is living on your day-to-day teaching as if it is all he has, rather than drawing on a large repertoire of known writing techniques and strategies.	Whenever I teach something, I love to see kids like you go off and give it a go. It means they are pushing themselves to try new things. But I also hope that isn't *all* kids do. We've talked about how writers carry invisible backpacks full of strategies. When I teach a minilesson, I give you something new to add to your backpack, but it is important to use everything else you have in there too! Today, I want to teach you one way writers remind themselves of what they already know about revision. They look at artifacts, like classroom charts and our Information Writing Checklist, and look back at old entries to remind themselves of the strategies they know. Then, they write an action plan.	Writers take action! 1. Look at charts, your notebook, and the Information Writing Checklist. 2. Make a list of the ways you could revise. 3. Create an action plan for yourself.

If . . .	After acknowledging what the child is doing well, you might say . . .	Leave the writer with . . .
The Process of Editing		
The writer has edited but has missed several mistakes or would otherwise benefit from learning to partner-edit. This writer often thinks she has written what she intended to say, and therefore she overlooks many mistakes. She would benefit from learning to edit with a partner before publishing her writing.	I know that you have worked hard to use many of the editing strategies you know and have made many changes to your piece. As a result, it is clearer and more readable. Sometimes as a writer, though, you know so clearly what you *wanted* to say that you miss places where you may have said something in a confusing or incorrect way. That's why most writers have editors that look at their writing once it's done. Today, I want to teach you a few things you and your writing partner can do together. You can: • Read your piece aloud and ask your partner to check to make sure what you say matches what he or she sees. • Circle words you think are misspelled and try to figure them out together. • Use the class editing checklist together.	A few things you and your writing partner might say to each other: • "Reread your piece, and I'll make sure what you say matches what I see." • "Let's circle the words that we think are misspelled and try them again." • "Let's use our class editing checklist to proofread your piece."

Opinion Writing

If . . .	After acknowledging what the child is doing well, you might say . . .	Leave the writer with . . .
Structure and Cohesion		
The introduction does not forecast the structure of the essay. The writer has made a claim and supported it with reasons, but there is no forecasting statement early on in the essay that foreshadows the reasons to come. Instead, it seems as if the writer thought of and wrote about one reason, then when reaching the end of that first body paragraph, thought "What's another reason?" and then raised and elaborated on that reason. He is ready to learn to plan for the overarching structure of his argument and forecast that structure in the introduction.	You have definitely learned to make a claim in your essay and to support that claim with reasons. There is one big step you need to take, though, and that is to let your reader know how your essay will go from the very beginning, in the introduction. Today, I want to teach you that opinion writers forecast how their writing will go. They do this by stating their claim in the introduction and then adding on, "I think this because. . . ." Then they list the reasons that they will write about in the body of their piece.	Writers use the introduction to forecast how their opinion pieces will go. 1. State your claim. • "I think . . ." 2. Tell your reader why your claim is true. • "One reason I think . . . is because . . ." • "Another reason I think . . . is because . . ." • "The final reason I think . . . is because . . ."
Supports are overlapping. In this instance, the writer has developed supporting reasons that are overlapping or overly similar. While this may pose few problems now, the writer will struggle when the time comes to find examples to support each reason (because the examples will be the same!). For example, if a student argues, "Dogs make the best pets," she may provide the following reasons: they like to play games, they cheer you up, and they are great at playing fetch. Playing fetch and playing games overlap, and you'll want to help this student find another, different reason why dogs are great pets.	Sometimes, when writers develop supporting reasons for their thesis, they find that one or more of them overlap. What I mean by this is that they basically say the same thing! Today, I want to teach you that writers look at their supporting reasons with a critical eye, checking to see if any overlap. One way they do this is by listing the examples they'll use for each paragraph. If some of the examples are the same, then the reasons are probably too similar!	Are your supporting reasons too similar? Test them to find out! Support _____ Example #1: Example #2: Support _____ Example #1: Example #2: Support _____ Example #1: Example #2:

If . . .	After acknowledging what the child is doing well, you might say . . .	Leave the writer with . . .
Supports are not parallel or equal in weight. This writer has developed a thesis and supports. While all the supports may support the writer's overall claim, they are not parallel. For instance, when arguing that "dogs make great friends," the writer may have suggested that this is because (A) they always listen to you, (B) they play with you, and (C) one time I was sad and my dog cuddled with me. Supports A and B are both reasons for or ways that dogs can make great friends. Support C is an example of *one time* a dog made a good friend. This writer needs help identifying places where one or more supports are not parallel and/or are not equal in weight to the others.	As a writer, you want each part of your essay to be about equal in weight. What I mean by this is that all your supports should prove your overall claim *and* they should be something you can elaborate on with several examples. Today, I want to teach you that writers look back over their supports and ask, "Are these all equal in size?" One way they test out this question is by checking to see if they can give two to three examples for each support. If they can't, they have to revise the supporting reason to make it bigger.	Do you have examples to prove each of your supports? Support _____ Example #1: Example #2: Support _____ Example #1: Example #2: Support _____ Example #1: Example #2:
The writer is new to the writing workshop or this particular genre of writing. This writer struggles not because he has struggled to raise the level of his opinion writing, but because this is a new genre for him. He may display certain skill sets (e.g., the ability to elaborate or write with beautiful descriptions) but lacks the vision of what he is being asked to produce. His piece may be unfocused or disorganized. It also may be sparse, lacking any sort of elaboration.	As a writer, it can be particularly hard to write well if you don't have a vision, a mental picture, of what you hope to produce. Today, I want to teach you that one way writers learn about the kinds of writing they hope to produce is by studying mentor texts. They read a mentor text once, enjoying it as a piece of writing. Then, they read it again, this time asking, "How do opinion pieces seem to go?" They label what they notice and then try it in their own writing.	Writers use mentor texts to help them imagine what they hope to write. They: 1. Read the text and enjoy it as a piece of writing. 2. Ask, "How do opinion pieces seem to go?" 3. Label what they notice. 4. Try some of what they noticed in their own writing.
The writer has multiple, well-developed reasons, but they all blur together without paragraphs or transitions. This writer has developed multiple reasons to support his opinion and has supported those reasons with evidence. It is difficult to discern an organizational structure in the piece, however, because many of the reasons blur together without paragraphs or transitions.	A paragraph is like a signal to a reader. It says, "I just made an important point. Now I'm moving onto something else." Paragraphs give readers an opportunity to take in evidence part-by-part, reason-by-reason. Readers expect that opinion writers will separate their reasons in paragraphs, with one section for each reason. Writers reread their writing, take note of when they've moved from one reason to another, and insert a paragraph there.	Opinion writers use paragraphs to separate their reasons. Each paragraph has: Reasons + Evidence

If . . .	After acknowledging what the child is doing well, you might say . . .	Leave the writer with . . .
The writer is ready to consider counterarguments. This writer has shown evidence that she is ready to consider counterarguments. She may have written something like, "I know that not everyone agrees, but . . ." or may have gone further and laid out the opposing argument that others might make. She is ready to learn to use counterarguments to bolster her own argument.	You are doing one of the hardest things there is to do when you are working to write an argument. You are imagining the people who might disagree with you and trying to see an opposite point of view from your own. Today, I want to show you how to raise the level of that work by teaching you to use counterarguments to *make your own argument stronger!* One way to do this is by showing that there are flaws or gaps or problems in the counterargument, and then show how *your* argument addresses those problems. So you might start by saying, "This argument overlooks . . ." or 'This argument isn't showing the full story."	Strong opinion writers expose the flaws, gaps, and problems in counterarguments and then show how their argument addresses those problems. They might begin: • "This argument overlooks . . ." • "This argument isn't showing the full story."
Elaboration		
The writer is struggling to elaborate. (1) This writer has an opinion, as well as several reasons to support that opinion, but most reasons are stated without elaboration. He may have created a long list of reasons to support his opinion, but does not say more about any one reason or provide examples or evidence to support his reasons.	You know that when you give an opinion, you need to support it with reasons! But opinion writers don't just stop with reasons. Today, I want to teach you that when writers come up with a reason to support a claim, they then try to write a whole paragraph about that reason. One way to do this is by shifting into a mini-story. You can start your claim and reason and then write, "For example, one day . . ." or "For example, in the text . . ." and tell a mini-story that shows and proves your reason.	One way writers elaborate on a reason is by providing a mini-story to prove their point. They might write: • "For example, one day . . ." (personal essay) or • "For example, in the text . . ." (literary or argument essay)
The writer is struggling to elaborate. (2) This writer has an opinion, as well as several reasons to support that opinion, but most reasons are stated without elaboration. She may have created an endless list of reasons to support her opinion, but does not say more about any one reason or provide examples and evidence to support it. She has learned to use mini-stories to support her reasons and is ready for a larger repertoire of evidence.	You know that when you give an opinion, you need to support it with reasons! But opinion writers don't just stop with reasons. They need evidence to convince their readers that their claim is right. Today, I want to teach you that when writers come up with reasons to support a claim, they then try to write a whole paragraph about that reason. One way to do this is by adding facts, statistics, definitions, and quotes that support your reason. Writers have to choose the evidence that makes the most sense for them.	Opinion writers support reasons using: • Mini-stories • Facts • Statistics • Definitions • Quotes
The writer's evidence feels free-floating or disconnected from the argument at hand. This writer has elaborated on reasons using evidence but has done little to explain that evidence to his reader. He'll often drop a fact or statistic into a paragraph and may even recognize that it feels awkward. He needs strategies for elaborating on evidence, specifically by learning to tie it back to the overarching claim.	You have elaborated by providing not only reasons to support your claim, but evidence as well. Sometimes, when writers write persuasively, they incorporate facts and statistics and mini-stories, only to find that they feel awkward or disconnected from their own writing. Writers have a trick to fix this problem, and that is what I want to teach you today! One way writers make evidence particularly persuasive is by saying a bit about how that evidence relates to their claim. They might say, "This proves . . ." or "This shows that _____ is true because. . . ."	Writers don't just toss evidence into an opinion piece. Instead, they help their readers understand why it is there! They can help explain the importance of the evidence by writing things like: • "This proves . . ." • "This shows that ____ is true because . . ."

If . . .	After acknowledging what the child is doing well, you might say . . .	Leave the writer with . . .
The piece is swamped with details. This writer is attempting to be convincing and knows that details matter. Her writing is riddled with facts, details, quotes, and other forms of evidence in support of her thesis. Because the writing is so detail-heavy, the writer has likely struggled to fully integrate the evidence or explain it to her reader.	You are the kind of writer who knows that details matter. Today, I want to teach you that choosing the just-right details and cutting others can make your piece even better. One way to know what details to keep and what details to cut is to read each piece of evidence and ask, "Is that evidence the *most* convincing evidence I can give to convince my readers of my opinion?" Then you make some hard choices—keeping the best evidence and cutting the rest.	Opinion writers choose evidence carefully and critically! • Look at each piece of evidence and ask, "Is that evidence the *most* convincing evidence I can give?" • Then, keep the best evidence and cut the rest.
The writer has provided evidence, but it does not all support the claim. This writer has elaborated on his reasons with a variety of evidence, but not all of this evidence matches the point he is trying to make. It may be that a mini-story is unfocused and not angled to support a particular point. It may be that a quote or statistic does not connect directly to the claim. Either way, this writer needs help rereading his piece with a critical lens, checking to be sure that each sentence he has written helps to further his opinion.	As a writer, you know it is important not just to give a bunch of reasons for a claim, but also to spend time *proving* those reasons. You have already done this by including all sorts of evidence. Today, I want to teach you that after collecting evidence, writers go back to look at their writing with a critical lens. They ask, "Does this piece of evidence match my reason? Does it really prove what I am trying to say?" If it matches, they keep it. If not, they cut it out.	Opinion writers ask: • Does this piece of evidence match my reason? • Does this prove what I am trying to say? • If so, they keep it! If not, they cut it!
Language		

The writer uses a casual, informal tone when writing.
 	
As you read this writer's opinion pieces, you are overwhelmed by a sense of casualness and informality. Likely this comes from a good place on the writer's part. She may be trying to communicate directly with her audience. ("Hey, wait! Stop and think before you throw that piece of garbage on the ground.") She may also be attempting to be convincing. ("Littering is *sooooo* bad for the environment and kills animals every day!!") There is nothing wrong with this, but you sense that this writer is ready to move toward more sophisticated forms of persuasion, beginning with the adoption of a more formal, academic tone.
	As an opinion writer, your first and foremost job is to convince readers that your claim, your opinion, is correct. When you first start out as a persuasive writer, you learn fun little ways to do this, like talking to the reader or making exaggerations. But as you grow as a writer, the challenge becomes, "How do I make my writing equally as persuasive but do it in a way that sounds more sophisticated, more professional, more grown up?" Today, I want to teach you a few tricks for adopting a more formal tone in your writing. When writers want to sound more formal they:
	
	• Use expert vocabulary.
	
	• Use sophisticated transition words and phrases.
	
	• Incorporate startling facts from credible sources.
		Sound like an expert!
		
		• Use expert vocabulary related to your topic.
		
		  Example: When talking about the environment you might use words like *biodegradable* or *ozone*
		
		• Use sophisticated transition words to introduce insights, ideas, or examples.
		
		  Examples: *alternately, additionally, furthermore*
		
		• Incorporate startling facts from credible sources.
		
		  Example: "You may not have known that, according to recycling-revolution.com, recycling one aluminum can saves enough energy to power a TV for three hours!

If . . .	After acknowledging what the child is doing well, you might say . . .	Leave the writer with . . .
The writer struggles with spelling. This writer's piece is riddled with spelling mistakes. This does not necessarily mean the writing is not strong (in fact, the essay he wrote may be very strong), but the spelling mistakes compromise the reader's ability to understand it. The writer's struggle with spelling may stem from various causes—difficulty with understanding and applying spelling patterns, a limited stock of high-frequency words, lack of investment, the acquisition of English as a new language—and diagnosing the underlying problem will be an important precursor to teaching into it.	When an opinion piece (or any piece of writing, really) is full of spelling mistakes, it can be hard for readers to understand what you are trying to say. Today, I want to remind you that writers try out multiple ways to spell a word before settling on one. Then, if they are still stuck, they consult a friend, writing partner, word wall, or other classroom resource.	Writers work hard at their spelling. They: 1. Try multiple versions of a word in the margin. 2. Pick the one that looks right. 3. Consult a peer, word wall, or other resource to help.

The writer struggles with comma usage.
 	
This writer is attempting to form more complex sentences but is struggling with the process. It may be that she uses commas incorrectly, interspersing them throughout the piece with little rhyme or reason, or that she simply doesn't use commas, resulting in long, difficult-to-read sentences. Either way, this writer needs help understanding the ways commas are used in sentences.
	I've noticed that you've been trying to write longer, more complex sentences. Because of this, your writing sounds more like talking. It is quite beautiful. When writers write sentences that are more complex, though, they often need to use commas. Commas help readers know where to pause and help the sentence make sense. Today, I want to teach you a few important ways that writers use commas. Writers use commas in lists, to separate two or more adjectives, before (and sometimes after) names of people, and to separate two strong clauses that are separated by a conjunction.	Use commas:
		
		• To separate items in a list.
		  Example: I want pears, apples, and oranges.
		• To separate adjectives.
		  Example: He drove by in his red, shiny car.
		• Before and after names of people.
		  Example: My brother, Peter, is a good friend.
		  Example: John, don't be so silly!
		• To separate two strong clauses that are separated by a conjunction.
		  Example: I am working hard, but she is resting on the couch.
		  Example: She is taking an afternoon nap, and then we will go out for dinner.

If . . .	After acknowledging what the child is doing well, you might say . . .	Leave the writer with . . .
The Process of Generating Ideas		
The writer struggles to generate meaningful topics worth exploring. This writer feels stuck and has difficulty generating ideas for writing. Sometimes this manifests through avoidance behaviors (going to the bathroom, sharpening pencils), and other times the child simply seems to be in a constant state of "thinking," not writing. This child needs help not only with generating ideas but also with learning to independently use a repertoire of strategies when stuck.	I've noticed that coming up with ideas has been hard for you and that you've had to spend a lot of time thinking about what to write. When you write opinion pieces, you want them to be persuasive. And for them to be persuasive, you have to *care* a lot about the topic! It can help to think about what you really care the most about—think about things you love or hate—and then see if you can write opinion pieces about that.	Write what you love, write what you hate, but not about topics that fall in between.
The writer is exploring opinions that are overly simple or without dimension. This writer's notebook is full of entries about topics that are safe and relatively one-sided. If writing about his own life, he may be writing about how he loves his brother or how candy is the best treat. When writing about texts, the writer is apt to pick simple, obvious points to argue. Based on the work you see this child doing on a regular basis, you are sure that he is capable of developing more complex theses—those that take into account various points of view or that argue claims that are more difficult to prove.	You have been writing about clear, concise opinions like "Dogs make the best pets" and "My mom is my best friend." Today, I want to show you how to raise the level of the thinking work you are doing by raising the level of your thesis. One way to do this is by picking an issue that people have different opinions on. You can write first to explore one side of the argument, and then write to explore the other side.	Writers make their ideas more complex by exploring issues with multiple sides. "On the one hand, people think . . ." "On the other hand, people think . . ."
The Process of Drafting		
The writer has a clear plan for her writing but loses focus and organization when drafting. This writer seemed to have a clear structural plan for her writing. She went into the process with folders full of evidence or neatly sorted booklets. But, as she began drafting, all this organization seemed to fly out the window. That is to say, this writer put pen to paper and wrote, wrote, wrote—leaving behind any thoughts of groupings and paragraphs.	As opinion writers, it is important to make an argument in a clear, organized way. This allows the reader to follow what you are saying point by point. To create an organized argument, opinion writers make sure they rely on the plans they've created. It often helps to draft each part of your essay on a separate piece of paper, dedicating a new sheet to each reason. Then, when you are finished, you paste it all together.	Writers don't leave their plans behind! One way to make sure your drafts stay organized is to draft each section of your essay on a separate sheet of paper. Use a new sheet for each reason, and then paste the pages together at the end.

If . . .	After acknowledging what the child is doing well, you might say . . .	Leave the writer with . . .
The Process of Revision		
The writer has a limited repertoire of revision strategies. This writer lives off of each day's minilesson. He is task-oriented and generally applies (or attempts to apply) what you teach each day. This writer may work hard to revise, but when asked what else he might work on, he struggles to answer the question. This student is living on your day-to-day teaching as if it is all he has, rather than drawing on a large repertoire of known writing techniques and strategies.	As a writer, it is important that you take control of your own writing life. Writers use all they know about revision to make their pieces stronger. One way writers push themselves to get even stronger at writing is by studying mentor texts. They look at texts that resemble the kind they hope to create, find places that seem powerful and convincing, and then ask themselves, "What has the writer done to make these parts so powerful and convincing?" Then they try out the same in their own writing.	Writers study mentor authors to help them revise. They: 1. Study a piece that resembles the kind they hope to create. 2. Find places that seem powerful and convincing. 3. Ask, "What has the writer done to make these parts so powerful and convincing?" 4. Try the same in their own writing.
The Process of Editing		
The writer "edits on the run," investing little time or effort in the process. This writer is not applying what she knows about spelling, grammar, and punctuation while writing. It may be that you have taught a particular spelling pattern, and she mastered it in isolation but is not using that knowledge during writing workshop. She may also spell word wall words wrong or other words that are known (or easily referenced). There is often a sense that the writer does not care about the editing process, viewing it as a cursory last step before publication.	One thing I'm noticing is that editing goes awfully quickly for you and that many times you skip over mistakes. I've even seen you misspell a few words that are right up here on our word wall! Today, I want to teach you that editing is a multistep process and something that writers have to take seriously. One way to focus all your attention on editing is to pick one lens first—let's say ending punctuation—and read through your piece looking *only* for places where you need to add ending punctuation. Then you pick a second thing to look for, like checking to make sure all your tos, twos, and toos are correct. And again, you read through looking for only those mistakes. Writers do this until they've made it through the entire editing checklist.	Writers take each item on the editing checklist *one by one.* Editing checklist: • Read, asking, "Will this make sense to a stranger?" • Check the punctuation. • Do your words look like they are spelled correctly?